DESIGN MATTERS //

PACKAGING[01]

AN ESSENTIAL PRIMER FOR TODAY'S COMPETITIVE MARKET

CAPSULE

BEVERLY MASSACHUSETTS

ROCKPORT PUBLISHERS

First published in the United States of America by

Rockport Publishers, a member of

Quayside Publishing Group

100 Cummings Center

Suite 406-L

Beverly, Massachusetts 01915-6101

Telephone: (978) 282-9590

Fax: (978) 283-2742

www.rockpub.com

Library of Congress Cataloging-in-Publication Data

Design matters : packaging 01 an essential primer for today's competitive market.

　　p. cm.

　ISBN 1-59253-342-6

　1. Packaging--Design. I. Capsule (Firm)

　TS195.4.D48 2008

　　658.5'64--dc　　　　　　　　　　　　22 2008002187

　　　　　　　　　　　　　　　　　　　　　　　　CIP

ISBN-13: 978-1-59253-342-8

ISBN-10: 1-59253-342-6

10 9 8 7 6 5 4 3 2 1

Design: CAPSULE

Printed in China

Contents

pack•age (pak´ij) *verb*

to make into a package; especially: to produce as an entertainment package b: to present (as a product) in such a way as to heighten its appeal to the public.

ORIGIN 1540, "the act of packing," from pack (*n.*) or from cognate Du. pakkage "baggage." The main modern sense of "bundle, parcel" is first attested 1722. The verb is 1922, from the noun.

TO OUR FELLOW ARTISTS, PURVEYORS, DESIGNERS, FINANCIERS, AND INTERESTED PARTIES.

Design has arrived. Semantically package it how you like, but design is on the sharp edge of our future. As designers, we transform raw commodities into refined consumable goods—no matter how "good" they are. Modern cultures define themselves by the manner and quantity of items they consume. Now, we define consumption broadly. It isn't just the items that pass our lips heading for darker parts, it is anything for which we take ownership through our senses. The growing public has a thirst for designed consumables, and we are here to fill the trough. But how much consumption is too much?

As designers we have a responsibility and an opportunity to lead our consuming societies by their collective nose rings. Be it moral obligation or a duty to greater good, we must define a higher place for our trade. If we believe design to be an influential tool when we speak to clients and prospects, promising our results, why do we lack an oath to "do no harm"? We use the power of design to create a new reality but have no guide for the boundaries for achieving this new reality.

Capsule believes in profession and practice, words describing a higher obligation to smarter solutions. Our opportunities at Capsule have passed beyond our original imagination and we've been challenged to find new horizons and dreams for growth. We have balanced our opportunities with responsible thinking, hoping to advance our collective trade to its next evolution. We consider ourselves professionals living up to those who have given us training and striving to "do no harm" while achieving sustainable results for our clients, their clients, and the larger consuming public.

Design responsibly. Consume sustainably. Live extemporaneously. Thank you for reading, listening, and understanding.

Thank you,

Brian Adducci

Aaron Keller

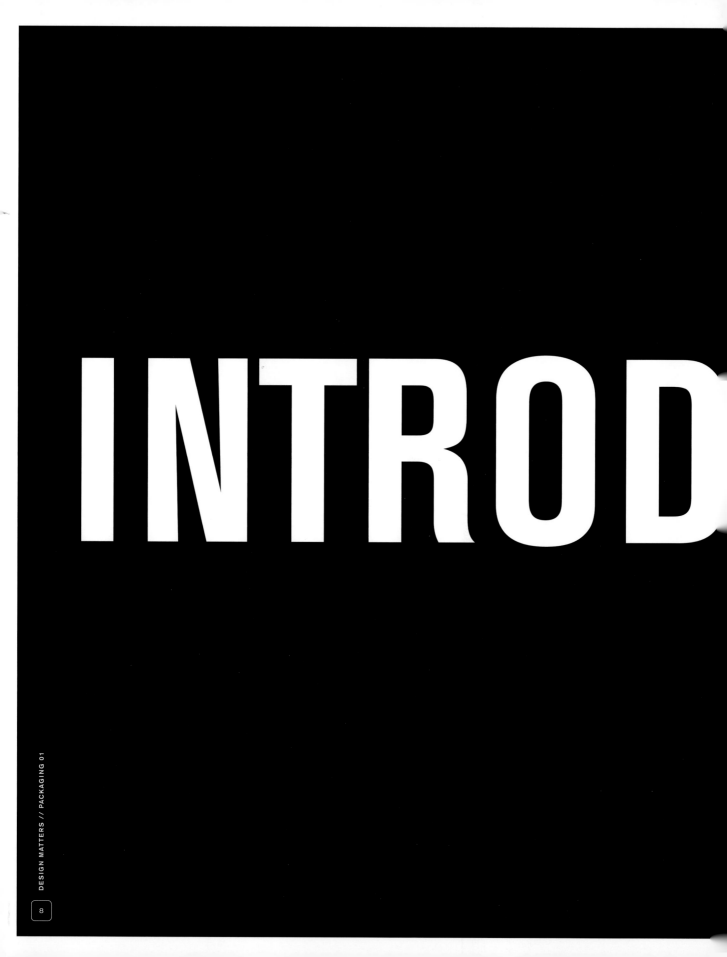

INTROD

UCTION

"THE ONLY FACTOR BECOMING SCARCE
IN A WORLD OF ABUNDANCE IS
HUMAN ATTENTION." – KEVIN KELLY

CUPPING TWO HANDS TOGETHER IN A RIVER. LIFTING WATER, THE SOURCE OF LIFE. PLUNGING YOUR FACE IN, TAKING A SIP. CONSUMING THIS PLENTIFUL PRODUCT, PACKAGED IN TWO HANDS. THE ORIGINAL, HIGHLY ORGANIC, RECYCLABLE, SUSTAINABLE, REUSABLE, AND MULTIPURPOSE PACKAGE DESIGN–YOUR RIGHT AND LEFT HAND.

The World of Packaging

Artifacts that are converted from natural resources to products often need to be packaged for safety, security, identification, containment, shipping, and all that surrounds the effort to get the resource from one place to another.

Packaging, defined holistically, is ubiquitous. Name something that doesn't come in a package. Not much comes to mind. Even an apple is labeled—a form of packaging. Your next pair of fashionable jeans will have at least one tag. Although packaging has been around since the birth of humanity, we are now starting to comprehend the impact packaging has on the planet we occupy.

After turning the last page of this book, you should have a better understanding of the intricacies of packaging, the process for creating it, and how it influences our world. But with new knowledge, questions arise and make you wonder, was the package discovered or invented?

Why We Package

SEE A NEED, PACKAGE A NEED

INTRODUCTION

At a basic level, we package to protect, contain, and identify products and materials from point A to point B. Sometimes that's the extent of what the package does. More often, there are other objectives behind why a product gets a package. These might include the vast number of specific marketing objectives to render a competitor helpless or take a step in the direction of a clear competitive advantage. Or perhaps a product needs to be kept until consumption or at a certain temperature until it reaches a final destination. And, of course, the objective may be to

We package because we need to; how we package is up to each of us. Asking the "how" and "why" questions are good starting points for any packaging design process.

protect it from kleptomaniacs getting their fix while getting away with your goods. We package for many reasons—with most objectives prioritized based on the contents and the intended audience or consumer.

So how important is the package to the eventual success of the product and brand? That depends on the relative importance of the contents and the importance you and your client place on the package design. Famed American psychologist Abraham Maslow, bless his heart, and his hierarchy of needs can provide a framework for considering a package's importance. Items that deliver on the physiological—the basic needs of an individual—will likely be packaged at the same level. The average, semi-lean, hamburger meat at the local grocery store, labeled and shrink-wrapped, is a great example of the way contents and package delivers on the physiological needs of a consumer. From base to peak, the self-actualization level is required to connect a product to these higher needs in a consumer's life. Compare semi-lean hamburger to the line of Donald Trump meats and we have a clear spectrum from physiological to self-actualization.

PHYSIOLOGICAL

The package
contains all parts
and documentation
for use of product
including ingredients,
recipes, and other
fundamental pieces.

SAFETY

The package protects
the product as well as
reduces theft or loss.

BELONGING

The package
presents the brand
and product in a way
that connects with a
larger community of
like-minded individuals,
making the connection
between individual
and community.

ESTEEM

The package delivers
the confidence,
competence, and
achievement of the
brand and connects
with the consumer
through highly
emotional methods.

SELF-ACTUALIZATION

The package turns
benefits into emotional
rewards surrounding
the brand and
the experience of
having the brand in
a consumer's life.

*The value of the package relative to the product inside changes as the product moves up
the hierarchy of needs. The diagram showcases some packages that exemplify this idea.
1) Physiological: hamburger meat package, one pound, 2) Safety: Microsoft clamshell
by Laura Coe Wright, 3) Belonging: mymy by Smith + Milton, 4) Esteem: M Vodka by Fitch,
5) Self-actualization: method surface cleaner by method*

SOURCE: CAPSULE

Packaging History

WE CONSUME, THEREFORE WE ARE

Consider the history of packaging and you must consider the history of how products reached consumers. As only two outlets existed just over 100 years ago—direct to consumer and a general store or village shop—packaging operated within this context. Packaging was a delivery device that was intended to get the product safely to its destination. Merchants offered the final hand delivery to the consumer seeking to make a purchase. Then Sears, Roebuck and Company, Marks & Spencer, and other national retailers brought us into the modern age of consumption-driven retail.

When we moved from a production-driven society to a consumption-driven society, packaging design became an essential part of the evolution. As new technologies and materials became available, the possibilities in design expanded drastically. Now that we live in this consumption-driven society, the package has become an essential identifier of our ability to consume. Just visit your local antique dealer before a trip to a modern retail store to see a mere hundred years' of change.

Digging deeper into the details, packaging existed to transport and protect a product while en route to its destination. In some categories of household products, the bulk packages we know today were more common as consumers were expected to store in quantity and use portions. This efficient distribution method was common when general stores or village shops were the primary retail options. Compare this to bulk stores today and the similarities are interesting.

Further exploration of the influences of packaging design takes us to the surrounding media, materials, manufacturing, processes, and other innovations. Historically, packaging was the only medium available to build a product brand. Other than a couple magazines, national advertising media was sparse until radio and television reached full-market saturation. New materials brought lighter-weight packages, better protection from theft and spoilage, and advancements that would amaze the average person from the prior century. Manufacturing processes evolved from individual laborers packing each product to completely automated plants that produce and package as many items in a day as laborers would produce in a year.

As in every other aspect of national economies, change is constant while the speed and type of change can be influenced. Taking you back to an age-old grade school lesson, it's what we learn from history that gives us the proper perspective. We can influence the change we make and learn from what has happened to create the right change for our economies, planet, and people.

Left: Middle America, early 1900s, Ankeny, Iowa, USA—A general store offers shoppers the service of two store owners and a pet on security detail. Many products were packaged in bulk to be individually distributed to each consumer as they specified their needs.

Right: Historical packaging is a looking glass into the past. Seeing what was done gives us much more respect for how far we've come in packaging design.

Packaging Today

BEAUTY, .01 MILLIMETER DEEP, 3 BILLION CONSUMERS WIDE

With the materials we have now, and the new ones being invented every day, with efficient prototyping and manufacturing processes—and with an abundance of design talent globally—we live in wonderful times for packaging design.

The vast number of mediums available for a marketer to reach consumers has created a glut of messaging that often overwhelms or at least confuses consumers. With abundant opportunities, and as the importance of packaging becomes more obvious, the world is shifting in favor of it. So much so that Procter & Gamble believes the package is the first and almost always the last moment of truth before a purchase is made.

The changing media landscape creates more opportunity for packaging that works hard at the shelf to get attention and gain trust.

Drawing a picture of the past, then turning it around and looking forward into the future, we see potential paths. These are mere guideposts, not predictions of an unknowable future.

1. SIMPLICITY: Yes, customers are still busy and desire packages that are simple to buy and understand. Complicated is the enemy.

2. CONVENIENT QUALITY: People want speed and convenience, without sacrificing quality. Within ten to twenty seconds, shoppers make a

category decision at the shelf. Quality of package conveys quality of product. Imagery and design only have a second or two for success or failure.

3. GLOBALIZATION: This impacts the sourcing of products, market expansion opportunities, and the sourcing of services such as printing, prototyping, and manufacturing. Identifying the country of origin is often required on packages and is becoming a larger part of consumers' decision-making criteria.

4. NEW CONSUMER INFORMATION: Price comparison is mere table stakes. Now customers compare corporate ethics, country of origin, and environmental responsibility.

R~Earth packages fertilizer and compost made from organic sources. Any organic gardener knows the heart of a great organic garden is in the materials used within the soil.

BLOK DESIGN

Sometimes just a box is much more. Inside the Roameo package two parts come together to create the pet containment product. The entire package is a self-contained kit to keep Spot and Lucky within site of their parents.

CAPSULE

Mixing materials on a package creates both an interesting effect and practical benefits. The rubber used on the Effen bottle is an elegant example of how a package design balances form and function.

CAHAN & ASSOCIATES

Certain technology packaging needs to put the product on display, giving it the best chance to connect with a shopper. The Jawbone package design is a museum-style display of an accessory that looks more like jewelry than it does technology.

FUSEPROJECT

NOISE IS NOTHING

Jawbone®

Bluetooth + Noise Shield

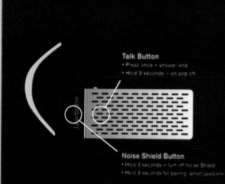

Talk Button
- Press once – answer/end
- Hold 3 seconds – on and off

Noise Shield Button
- Hold 3 seconds – turn off Noise Shield
- Hold 3 seconds for pairing when Jawbone off

Noise Shield Technology

- Jawbone's Noise Shield virtually eliminates all background noise from your call using military-grade audio processing technology.

- As your background noise environment changes, Jawbone seamlessly enhances your audio volume allowing you to hear your caller more clearly.

Wireless with Bluetooth

- Talk time: Up to 6 hours (when Noise Shield technology on)
- Standby Time: 200 hours
- Range: Up to 33 ft (10 meters)
- Compatible with Bluetooth version 1.1 or 1.2

*In modern packaging design, simplicity and restraint are
a coveted attribute for your sales person on the shelf.
This package (your sales person) confidently portrays the
bee as a unique identifier while still fitting into category
conventions for bottle shape and color.*

CAPSULE

The Benefit line of packages uses the contrast of color photography with black-and-white patterned backgrounds to create a modern yet historical feeling. The result is both elegant and stylish.

BENEFIT COSMETICA, LLC

Wally says it should be fresh, tasty, and beautiful. The package design is more an example of those three words than most things in our lives. It just makes you want to tear into those packages.

PHILIPPE BECKER DESIGN, INC.

5. BRAND TRUST: One million moments to build it and one moment to destroy it. Packaging can let consumers see inside the organization, and it requires trustworthy behaviors across all aspects of the organization.

6. GREEN IS THE NEW GOLD: Environmentalism and the new consumer are drawn to behaviors that preserve the planet we live on. Packaging design can make a large contribution to the fulfillment of this trend.

7. CONVERGENCE, SMERGENCE: Technology that combines multiple media into one device or moment, the Apple iPhone being the most prolific example known today. How does convergence impact packaging? When the package is an essential part of the product experience, we see another form of convergence.

8. MASS PERSONALIZATION: Products made for you, me, and the other guy in a way that feels like it was done one at a time but could really never be. The package design has great opportunities to bring mass customization to life on the package. The underwater art of this iceberg has yet to be discovered.

9. ME-SERVICE: People are smart, crowds are not. Getting one person through a self-check-out isn't much of a challenge, but when the crowd shows up, your new technology better be ready. As self-service shows up all over the packaged world, you'll find the design must be simplified, again and again and again.

10. EVERYONE'S A HILTON: Luxury isn't just reserved for the upper crust. Today's consumers buy small moments of luxury through the products and services they purchase. Design can create luxury for the masses and packaging to match.

11. ÜBER SPEED RETAIL: Step behind the scenes of a major retailer and you'll find yourself on a merry-go-round moving at light speed. The neo-retailers require a level of speed unknown to most consumers and likely alien to the average Jamaican.

12. RFID: "Ready for Identity Detection" is coming to visit you wherever you are. Yes, it is better known as Radio Frequency Identification Devices, which is quickly becoming the technology used to track where each and every package is from the supply chain to your home. Unlike other ingredients, you won't be able to say, "I'd like that without any RFID, please."

The Consumer Movement

RETHINKING THE WAY WE CONSUME

We would be forgetting something if we failed to look through consumers' eyes to see the world through a new pair of green-tinted glasses. As designers, we sit in creative sessions and talk about utopian worlds, but we need to bring the average consumer along to this new responsible community for it to be truly sustainable.

So where does the consumer come in? First, stop and look around, and take a visual inventory of your life. Where did everything come from? Where will it end up? How can you consume the artifacts in your life and in the lives of your children more efficiently? From transportation to materials to behaviors, take a closer look at how you live. You may find little things that seemed embarrassingly cheap before now seem smart and frugal.

Start with a change in perception of what is "cool" and add a fourth R to the list: recycle, reuse, reduce, and regift. We've all heard of it. Many have done it. Just remember to take out the note from Aunt Betty before regifting a wedding present to your long-lost college roommate. Consider the savings in transportation, packaging, and materials when we recognize that one person's well-intentioned but misguided gift is another person's prized possession. If products that are better for the environment feel like they are less than equal because of unique or simplified packaging, take another look. You might find a change in perspective can change a bad gift into a great idea for the environment.

We need to wake up the minds of consumers wandering through their shopping list. Give them a reason to whisper, "Oh, what's this?" Designers have the opportunity, and some might say an obligation, to make package designs compelling, appealing, and even sexy to the environmentally conscience consumer. This seems to be the exact mission of the product designers behind Ecoist.com. Make it fashionable to reuse old candy wrappers and we might be on to something. We might actually have a design-driven, economically sustainable shift in thinking and behavior. Let's make it a collective "we." Let's make it competitive. Let's make it economical. Let's make it last. Let's lead the way. Many will follow.

These wrappers were designed for another purpose but are now extending the useful life of the package and creating something beautiful from a plentiful resource— pre-consumer waste packaging.

LUNA AND ECOIST.COM

Seeing can facilitate understanding, and seeing the flow of resources through our global economy helps us see how many places in the process can be impacted by design.

GREENBLUE

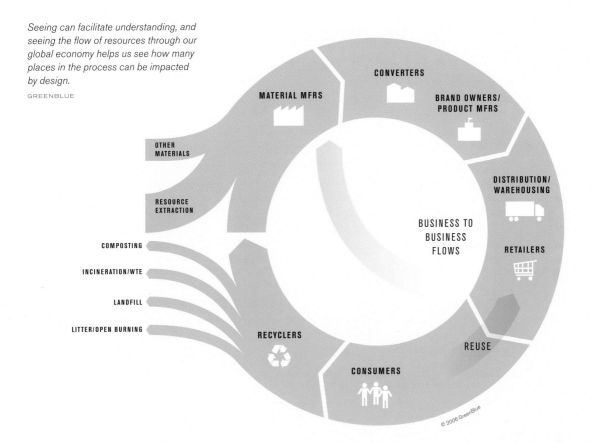

MATERIAL MFRS

CONVERTERS

BRAND OWNERS/
PRODUCT MFRS

OTHER
MATERIALS

RESOURCE
EXTRACTION

DISTRIBUTION/
WAREHOUSING

BUSINESS TO
BUSINESS
FLOWS

COMPOSTING

INCINERATION/WTE

LANDFILL

LITTER/OPEN BURNING

RETAILERS

RECYCLERS

REUSE

CONSUMERS

© 2006 GreenBlue

Finished with your Pangea product? Plant the package in your backyard, add water, and wait for the results to sprout from the ground.

IDEO

PANGEA
ORGANICS

BAR SOAP

EGYPTIAN FENNEL WITH
GRAPEFRUIT & SWEET ORANGE

Globalization

BRANDS WITHOUT BORDERS

The globalization of packaging design brings to mind the movie *The Gods Must Be Crazy,* released in 1980 with the drop of a Coke bottle on a small Botswana village in Africa. Likely the most ubiquitous package and surely the most common brand name known to the masses, the Coke bottle takes on new meaning in the village. This interesting perspective should create a few thoughts in a packaging designer's head, one being, "Where will this package be in the world?" The other questions may include, "Could this be used as a weapon?" Or just, "How else might this package be used?"

As our global community is in many different stages of change and evolution, we see how just the concept of a packaged product may mean something completely different to someone else. Although the humor is fun, the impact is serious. Consideration of a global community means we see beyond our own selfish shores

Overcoming the challenges of a global package design will likely bring rewards in distribution, cultural knowledge, and eventually sales.

to adopt the perspective of others without pity. Pity is a highly emotional response, and the design community swims in the warmest pools of emotion, making it particularly hard to manage. Some just ignore it and others don't care. The best have dealt with the emotional adjustment and view other people on the planet as equals no matter where they are on a perceived socio-economic scale.

The fundamentals of globalization cover languages, graphics, visuals—and the need to adapt to each country or region. How much adaptation takes place depends on the globalization strategy of the organization. Some organizations,

such as IKEA, make no apologies for product names that sound unusual in the English language. IKEA takes a country of origin approach and expects the shopper to learn, adapt, and understand. At the other end of the spectrum, Coca-Cola adapts a fair amount to each country and language with product graphics, lettering, and other package attributes. Neither is right or wrong, but each represents a different organizational strategy to globalization.

Once a strategy is set, the most important next step is for the designers to research possible meanings around all aspects of the package. The meaning of colors, images, words, phrases, typefaces, and shapes can change by country, region, or culture. This doesn't mean the winning package adapts to everyone. Sometimes strange translations can convey authenticity when it comes to an international product package. On the other side, the risk of offending needs to be understood, hence knowledge of meaning is essential. With knowledge, specific tactics can be mapped out and potholes can be avoided. Global packages can reap global rewards but they also have global obligations.

Spend time looking at the Coca-Cola bottles from around the world, and they reveal a global strategy of adaptation. The shape of the bottle holds the key to global consistency while the visual language adapts.

PLANNI

NG

"TO ACQUIRE KNOWLEDGE, ONE MUST STUDY; BUT TO ACQUIRE WISDOM, ONE MUST OBSERVE."
— MARILYN VOS SAVANT

START BROAD, GO NARROW, AND THEN FAN OUT AGAIN. PUSH A LARGE RIVER THROUGH A NARROW CANYON AND YOU MOVE BOULDERS. LIKE A RIVER, THE PACKAGING DESIGN PROCESS NEEDS TO FLOW FROM WIDE OPEN TO NARROW AND THEN BACK TO WIDE AGAIN.

The Flow of a Process

Starting broad means seeking to understand all aspects of the category where the package will reside. Moving on with secondary research, then to the primary research, and finally to anything you can get your clammy mitts on will help you gain the global perspective of your packaging endeavor.

Now, start to narrow the river of knowledge. Get to the essential items that will help define what this product and package will mean to consumers. Seek specific answers to specific questions and the river of knowledge will start to narrow itself. Pieces will fall away and others will become much more important. The creative energy around certain aspects will start to move aside the mental boulders, and ideas will start to surface. The idea is continually refined until it becomes a gem floating atop the river. This gem of an idea inspires many other ideas that flow directly out of this intense ideation process. Ideas are engineered, tested, and further refined until they reach a point of execution and delivery, all of which are dependent upon the talented people involved.

The cadre of individuals who explore new territory is always better when equipped with diverse skills and perspectives. Following the river metaphor, no one would rationally choose to be accompanied by rocket scientists on a white-water rafting trip, right? Nothing against rocket scientists, but can they swim, handle a paddle, or fight back the wildlife? Having them around might be fun, but what you really want is a bona fide guide. You need someone with muscle, a map reader, and even a happy observer who can simply watch for rocks to avoid—multidisciplined, multiskilled, and multitalented.

With a budget in hand, as well as clear objectives and the right catalyst, your process has begun. We'll work out the details as we go.

Research

METHODS FOR MADNESS OR BRILLIANCE

In the last decade, research methods for packaging have seen a number of technological and creative advances. These advances allow a marketing manager to set up tracking studies to see how a shopper eyes a package or an entire category. Other creative methods get at the underlying psychology behind the decision a shopper makes by inviting them to create collages depicting your brand as it relates to their life and talking at length about relevant metaphors and emotional factors. Going even farther, current research techniques by Dan Hill read emotional reactions to visual language, translating the ever-elusive emotional landscape of consumers. With so many methods for and perspectives on how to understand the shopper, it's easy to get wide-eyed and walk right past the fundamentals of research. Seeking to understand people, culture, and objects is the

baseline—from here you should build a plan to gain that understanding while keeping any biases in check.

Context is essential. When observing behaviors, asking questions, or just getting a feel for the situation, having the right context matters. What does this mean when it comes to packaging? It translates to: "Where will your package live its life?" Research in consumers' homes will likely reveal certain behaviors and influences when it comes to the packaging they prefer. Research in retail will get at other aspects. These are the big areas, but by no means the only ones. How does the package translate at work, in the car, on the bus, or waiting for the train? Some contexts matter more than others, obviously, but they may surprise you with findings that impact the packaging design.

Objectives are next. The method of research varies from simple individual observation to multivariable analysis with an intentionally predictive outcome. This requires starting with a set of objectives that will drive your choice of methods and set context. Objectives should be measurable, but sometimes it's just good to write them down, measurable or not. Measurable objectives can cover you and your boss's rearview mirror, but sometimes they get in the way of seeking knowledge. It's hard to see the road ahead if you're always looking at what you left behind.

Exploratory research is the place to begin when looking at a package design process. This Texas-sized broad category of research contains everything from gathering secondary research from online sources to visiting the place where the package will eventually be displayed for sale.

Testing concepts in context can provide insights not readily grasped by just creating a design. Adapting the design based on research can improve the chances of success without diluting the original concept.

CAPSULE

Shoppers use fat percentages as an essential part of their milk buying decision. The Schroeder Milk package design uses this research knowledge to create a clean, simple package design. The result? An increase in sales, distribution, and shoppers who actually prefer Schroeder Milk products.

CAPSULE

Field interviews can take place after intercepting shoppers or recruiting them to a specific context (mall, store, home, etc). Using an experienced interviewer to ask open-ended questions can yield amazing insights into your package and how it performs in the chosen context. This method can be qualitative with a large enough sample size, but the real focus should be on the questions and the interviewer conducting the research. Fieldwork is essential for any brand with a package.

Testing is set up with assumptions and seeks to understand truths about how the larger population will respond to aspects of the package. Although highly valuable to understand consumer reactions in context, testing can also be one of the most overused methods next to focus groups for exploratory research. For instance, over-testing something to ensure that it doesn't offend anyone leads to a rather boring package design.

Facial recognition techniques explored by Dan Hill in his book, *Emotionomics,* offer a field full of amazing discoveries. Interpreting facial reactions allows you to see true emotions coming from consumers. The innovative techniques interpret visible reactions to better understand an emotional decision-making process. For example, try opening a bottle of curdled milk in front of a friend, smelling it, and then asking him to try it. Unless your friend has an odd fascination with spoiled food, he'll likely refuse with only a few words exchanged. Such techniques offer much more reliable, emotional information to inform packaging decisions.

Research is only as good as how it is implemented in setting strategy, informing creative, or redirecting an effort. Leveraging research sometimes means not doing anything at all and having enough confidence in the current plan to take no action. On the side of change, the right research can lead to significant advantages at the shelf. Having a better understanding of the consumer in certain contexts can be the tool to unseat a complacent competitor or stay ahead of the horde of new entrants.

By understanding the visual patterns in the category, the Sommerfield private label line of products can flex to candy, foods, and even baby products. Letting the food category lead creates opportunities to add category-specific personality within each product line.

TURNER DUCKWORTH

RESEARCH PLANNING

RESEARCH PLANNING: CHECKED TWICE, TRIANGULATED ONCE

Conducting research has many facets, opportunities, and painful realities. Using research to gain understanding is smart; using research simply to prove your point is dangerous. Start with a checklist and confirm your findings with triangulation.

1) What are you looking to understand?

2) Specifically, what is/are your objective(s) for the research?

3) What methods will be the most efficient?

4) What methods will have the least amount of bias, or where can bias be managed?

5) What level of confidence can you expect from the research?

6) What do you expect as an outcome?

7) What do you not want to see as the outcome? What are the implications of this?

8) Who will be researched? Who will be profiled? What individual or group of individuals?

9) How will you connect to them? How difficult or expensive will it be to research them?

10) How long will the research take? How does the time factor influence your market plan?

11) What will it cost? Will the knowledge gained be more valuable than the cost?

12) What else can the research be used for? Selling tool? Secondary report for sale?

Strategy

RATIONALIZE STRATEGY, EMOTIONALIZE DESIGN

Business strategy, brand strategy, experience strategy, channel strategy, creative strategy, retail strategy—insert a word in front of "strategy" and you've gained fifteen IQ points and a master's in business. Translating what you just said when a weathered and experienced entrepreneur says, "Son, what did you just say?" is when street IQ shows up. Strategy is just another word for applied knowledge: in other words, IQ points that have been earned, not purchased from business school. If we learn from experience, we should be able to set a better strategic course for the future.

Packaging is one of the essential places where a strategy comes to life and forms meaning with consumers. Packaging is often the result of many strategic paths to achieve set objectives. In other words, the longer a package has been on the shelf, the more likely it has traversed many strategic paths. Managed well, this can translate into a package connected to consumer culture and reflective of the brand strategy set forth by a capable management team. Managed poorly, the results are either obvious or become obvious when the nearest competitor takes advantage and translates the results into increased distribution, sales, and/or brand loyalty.

In the same way the operations team makes a large equipment purchase to create a new product, enter a new market, or increase efficiencies of an existing operation, the package design process should result in the creation of a custom built asset. This asset, if designed right, can be a strategic tool. The difference is contained in a rather large, scary, and gooey word—emotion. Although a double-duty, 65 percent more efficient, and 25 percent less expensive piece of equipment can be rationalized, a package design change is emotional. Even if we rationalize it with competitive case studies, it is still emotional. And it should be. Consumers buy emotionally in a way that seldom can be rationalized. The package design needs to be emotional, while also being rational. Thus is the intersection of business strategy and design methodology.

Design as a methodology for visualizing business strategy is not a new concept, as Walt Disney had an entrepreneurial grasp of the idea over half a century ago. It has been taken to new heights of awareness more recently by Procter & Gamble, Target, and Apple.

How does this translate to a packaging design process? Simple. Take equal parts strategy and design, blend them by a team of open-minded, educated individuals, and a strategy comes to life in the form of a package. Over-emphasize the business strategy and you'll end up with a litany of brand extensions with no design authenticity or rationale for that matter. Over-emphasize the design and you'll end up with a beautiful package without a single customer interested in buying it.

Balancing design and strategy creates an opportunity to appeal to unique, separate audiences—men and women—both of which are targets for this brand of sunglasses. The design creates an appealing solution to a smart strategy.

SUBPLOT DESIGN

No rational person would put wine in a solvent container, would they? Rational and emotional working in balance offers opportunities to see a new market of wine consumers, willing and proud to pour their wine from what could also be used for mineral spirits at your local hardware store.

KOREFE

PRIVATE LABEL BRANDS

With advancements in packaging technology and the cost of creating a package falling, the old black-and-white version of private labels is long gone. Today, many private label brands are not using the store brand name and have come close to equaling or surpassing the manufacturer's brand. ACNielsen recently studied private label brands globally and found that 69 percent of consumers believe private label goods are an extremely good value, and 62 percent think private labels offer quality that is equal to or greater than the big brands. This finding, along with the fact that 30 percent of Ahold's (a European-based grocery conglomerate) overall sales

come from private label and Sweden's ICA captures somewhere between 30 and 40 percent, means private label brands are an increasing competitive threat to stagnation.

How does private label packaging impact you? If you're representing a private label brand and find the product categories innovation challenged, you'll find an opportunity to capture more margin through private label programs. If you're representing a manufacturer's brand, innovation is one of the best battle-axes to keep out private label competitors.

Some retailers have taken the tactic of being a close follower of the national brand as an appropriate competitive behavior. Others have gone as far as designing a package that some might say fools the consumer when trying to decide at the shelf. This second tactic may offer short-term gains, but it fails to build trust with the consumer or the general population, and fails to establish a national brand, so in the long term, everyone loses.

RETAILER CONCENTRATION OF THE MOST DEVELOPED PRIVATE LABEL MARKETS

Country	Region	Private Label Share	Retailer Concentration
1. Switzerland	Europe	45%	86%
2. Germany	Europe	30%	65%
3. Great Britain	Europe	28%	65%
4. Spain	Europe	26%	60%
5. Belgium	Europe	25%	80%
6. France	Europe	24%	81%
7. The Netherlands	Europe	22%	64%
8. Canada	North America	19%	62%
9. Denmark	Europe	17%	89%
10. United States	North America	16%	36%

SOURCE: ACNIELSEN'S THE POWER OF PRIVATE LABEL 2005 REPORT

Private label growth correlates to retailer concentration and generally has the greatest penetration in European countries. The opportunities for private label packaging are growing at a substantial rate.

Waitrose private label packaging is designed in the most honestly beautiful manner. Simply showing the beauty of the individual products using a consistent design approach is a great example of the power of private label brands.

TURNER DUCKWORTH

Constraints

WHISPER SWEET DESIGNS TO ME, BABY

If necessity is the mother of invention, then constraint is your scholarly aunt. Set your boundaries and it becomes a matter of what can be done within the limitations. Set more boundaries and you'll be amazed by the results you achieve, whether you stick to the constraints or stretch the rules. Authentic creative behaviors thrive on constraints and become paralyzed by the blank page. Limitless opportunities are good; setting boundaries on creativity is better. What may seem like a paradox offers a perspective on fueling the creative process.

What makes constraints so helpful? It might be the comfort in having the requirements on the table and allowing the creative ideas to flow down a focused path. It might also be that we yearn for limitless opportunities but can't cognitively deal with infinite possibilities. The World Wide Web is an elegant example of what seems limitless, yet we navigate it with simplified search engines such as Google. Or consider how the complexities of computing and all the technology in our lives have been simplified by Apple's design. Constraints are all around us; acknowledging and understanding them is design's challenge and the place where it can shine.

Once you know that limits exist, the next step is identifying and articulating them. As a brand owner pontificates the vision for the brand and how the package must be the opening page of the brand story, design thinkers must interpret this message. Global, visionary speeches often sound like they don't have constraints, but listen harder and you'll hear key words that bring ideas into focus. What is the brand story? Does it have all the elements of a good novel or does it read like CliffsNotes? Who are the characters (sub-brands, partnerships, parent brand, etc)? Asking paired comparison questions can further define the constraints. Questions like, "Do you expect to see this package on the shelves in Seoul, South Korea, or Detroit, Michigan?" This type of question helps to form conceptual boxes for the design process. Generally, the more questions, the smaller the box becomes. And as my stepmother always said, "The smaller the box, the more valuable the contents."

Please, not another box on the shelf, anything but a box. Constrained to the efficiencies that come with said box, the Full Tank packaging design takes the box in an entirely new direction. Every detail is considered and given a role in communicating the brand personality.

TURNSTYLE

CREATIVE BRIEF

Putting words and visuals on paper—one to two pages at most—is what writing a creative brief is all about. The brevity of a brief—and identifying specific goals—is important. Done right, the brief gets better—and usually shorter.

Here are some of the fundamentals that should be included:

••• Background on the brand and the company behind the brand

••• Brand attributes (promise, personality, archetype, features, benefits, emotional rewards)

••• Distribution of the brand (types of retailers, international, countries, regions, etc)

••• Market research recently conducted and top findings from research

••• Trends or other external factors influencing the brand and package

••• Target audiences (purchaser, influencer in the decision, and end user of the product/package)

••• Timeline with critical dates and budget with hours broken out by critical dates

••• Production issues, structural parameters, and other constraints

••• Regulatory issues and environmental opportunities

CREATI

NG

"IF KNOWLEDGE CAN CREATE PROBLEMS,
IT IS NOT THROUGH IGNORANCE THAT
WE CAN SOLVE THEM." — ISAAC ASIMOV

RESTING ON THE SHELF, STANDING TALL FOR THE PASSERBY TO SEE. SETTING A STANDARD FOR THE CATEGORY OR HOPING TO BE NEARLY AS GOOD AS THE LEADING PACKAGE. HAVING CRITERIA TO JUDGE A PACKAGE, SETS THE BAR AT THE RIGHT HEIGHT.

Essential Criteria

Keeping up with the Joneses can be exhausting, especially when the Joneses continually redefine their style.

High jumpers set high bars. Low jumpers, well, low bars. What standards do you set against your work to judge it before the world does? Criteria are essential marks against your own expectations, those of the client, and most important, the final consumer. Set your bar low and consumers will respond with the same sad look given the lowest jumper at the end of an Olympic event.

The four criteria of a successful package are identification, functionality, personality, and navigation. Identification speaks to how well the consumer can identify the product from the package when shopping the category. Functionality relates to the usability of the product and increasing the product's purpose and efficacy. Personality is how the brand comes to life on the package. And navigation refers to how the consumer finds and uses the category and specifically, your selection of packages. All four criteria may not be amplified on one package, as some criteria are set higher depending on the strategy agreed upon by the brand management team.

The result is a package that is in balance with the strategy and, if well executed, has an increased chance to contribute to a successful product launch. Set your own standards, communicate them clearly, and then design a package to exceed those standards.

Criteria 1: Identification

TELL ME WHAT YOU SEE, DR. RORSCHACH

Seeing is believing, right? Wrong. Seeing, feeling, hearing, smelling, and touching are worth believing. What is the first thing you see when you glance at a product on the shelf? What does the package say about the product inside? Depending on the category, there are many elements that help identify the product within the category. These identifiers can be long-established conventions in a category or new revolutions in an ever-changing marketplace.

Conventions, like color or bottle shape, are used to identify wine bottles in the U.S. market but are not required by law. The shape, along with the color, tends to follow the grape variety. These "laws" of the category might as well come with a prison sentence when considering the career implications if they're disobeyed.

But what's with boxed wine? Old rules need not apply. Put wine in a TetraPak package, provide individual serving sizes, offer it to a more youthful consumer, and you've broken away to create a new category. The good news: With success you get to write the new category rules. The bad news: First you have to achieve success.

Identification sets the foundation for a good package design. If this criterion is misunderstood or not used appropriately, the first step into the marketplace will be a big misstep.

Understanding category conventions requires a talent for keen observation.

Shape, color, type, materials, and many other aspects of packaging can hold identification conventions that are essential to the category. Knowing these and why they exist gives you permission to bend the conventions that need bending. Permission is key. Just bending rules because

get bent. Consider laundry detergent refill bottles that remind us of all the ways to get soiled, but still look clean and almost clinical. This package design walks a fine line on the edge of the category and will therefore stand out on the shelf. Although each package contains the same ingredients, the multitude of refill packages tells a novel of a story instead of the abridged version usually told on laun-

Great package design takes a leap within the category, not completely out of the category and over a cliff.

it's fun would be akin to child's play and certainly irresponsible design decision-making. For instance, what comes to mind when considering laundry detergent? Clean, bright, disinfected clothing—hence, clean, bright, lively, colored packaging. This is a category norm that deserves to

dry detergent packages. The package engages consumers first with novelty, and once the environmental story is told, they have the first of many reasons to be loyal. If you're tired of the sanitized, edited, and narrow story told by most laundry detergent packages, then this is your next purchase.

The same product packaged in a variety of bottles tells a visual story and engages consumers with the brand.

KINETIC

By identifying a new, more youthful category of wine consumers, boxed wine can be cool and successful without conforming to the rules of the category.

CAHAN & ASSOCIATES

Criteria 2: Fuctionality

HELLO MR. FUNCTION CURMUDGEON

When does a package become an integral part of the product? When the functionality of the package reaches or exceeds that of the product it contains. The moment when the package adds emotional rewards or unexpected benefits to buying the product is when the line between product and package is blurred.

PLANNING | **CREATING** | IMPLEMENTING

MADE BY SCIENTISTS, NOT A SODA POP COMPANY

M MORNING · PUSH · POWER · GLUG

Pop the top, and pop your vitamins. Water infused with vitamins is finding its way into our lives. This package adds the functionality of enhancing your water just before you consume it, retaining the integrity of your vitamin consumption.

FORMATION DESIGN

The functional package design contributes to how the package will be accepted by essential audiences: the channel—distributor, buyer, and retailer—and the eventual product consumer. Because the function differs for the channel and the consumer, these two interests often conflict. The channel desires ease of transportation, restocking, efficient use of retail footprint, and many other operational efficiencies vital to cost containment. The consumer has vastly varied—almost too many to list—interests depending on the product category and their lifestyle. Highly functional design for a consumer is typically not in alignment with the interests of the channel participants. Intuitive designers should be able to find the overlaps and create exceptional design functionality for the essential audiences.

Understanding function means seeing dysfunction and being able to confidently identify it as such. You know it the moment you try to pick up a package without handles or open a container that takes three hands and a sharp tool. That's called dysfunction. The next step in educating your eyes is gaining the ability to identify exceptional function. Great functional design naturally becomes part of our life, as if it were meant to be there all along.

Seeking a competitive advantage to keep a pesky entrant out of your category? When done right, the packaging function will deliver on measurable business objectives. Functionality in a package can be stronger than changes to the product because it can alter how the product fits into someone's life. It can change behaviors, which a veteran marketer would say is like reaching the Holy Grail. Change how the package functions and you change how the consumer functions with it.

Having properly trained eyes and then a properly trained team to create function requires multiple disciplines. Designers, engineers, anthropologists, buyers, operations managers, and anyone who has passed the threshold of recognizing dysfunction and entered the world of articulating an elegant function should be included. Creating a new function or changing what exists needs to be handled by the properly experienced group—approaching it casually will likely result in casualties.

Integrating a tray into the paint container is both convenient and a simple reduction in resources needed for that weekend paint job.

FLEX/THE INNOVATIONLAB

EXERCISE: FOLLOW THE PACKAGE

In order to find new functional design possibilities, you need to see where the current package is functioning. So, follow it through its entire life cycle. Follow each step, without exceptions and without skipping. Have at least three people do this exercise at different times and journal as they go, taking note of what they see and any ideas that may have popped up.

The first thing you should acquire following this process is a large number of notes taken during the package's journey from origination to final disposal. Each stage should have notes from the three participants, whose ideas can be analyzed and findings summarized using all three in a pseudo-triangulation of results. Dig deep into the results and you'll find the places where additional functionality may serve a relevant and valuable purpose. Dig into frustrations and places where consumers got stuck with the package, and you'll likely find additional functions worth exploring.

In the end, you're not looking for a competitive advantage. You're looking for ways to surprise a consumer with additional function that eventually leads to a competitive advantage in packaging.

Convenience and function are much the same idea. For example, when does the package contribute to the convenience of the product? When the paint can becomes the holder and strainer for the paint roller, the convenience factor is amplified. This is where the idea of context becomes essential.

STANDARD PAINTING TOOLS: ▶

- One roller
- One gallon (3.8 L) paint
- One tray

STANDARD PROCESS OF PAINTING: ▶

- Open paint
- Pour paint
- Apply paint
- Repeat until finished
- Clean up tray and brush

FLEXA: PREMIUM PAINT BRAND: ▶

- Quality of any paint is hard to judge
- Private label brands are infringing
- Customer experience has seen little innovation
- Existing packaging offers little additional functionality

The discoveries to be found in contextual research are amazing. Seeing your package in the world where it lives will reveal many possible improvements to functional design. Evaluating which improvements are worthwhile is up to you and your team.

INNOVATIVE CONCEPTS DEVELOPED: ▶

▸ Solutions generated
▸ Technical requirements met
▸ Quality and durability met
▸ Logistics requirements achieved

CONCEPT REFINEMENT: ▶

▸ Ergonomics considered
▸ Environmental challenges addressed
▸ Visual language designed
▸ Functional specifications further defined

IMPLEMENTAION:

▸ Logistically sexy
▸ Functionally elegant
▸ Less waste of paint
▸ Less waste of trays
▸ More happy homeowners

Criteria 3: Personality

PRINCESS CONSISTENCY WILL RULE THE KINGDOM

Sell a boat, car, house, or any other high-ticket item, and you'll finish with a handshake. Sell baby cereal or a cell phone accessory, and the only personal interaction may be the package itself. When this is all you have, it is essential to deliver on brand personality.

The brand personality comes to life and delivers its largest impression the moment someone picks up the package. From this point, we have to think of the brand personality as an actual person. Now, who is this person? It can't be ten people, but it has to appeal to tens of millions of people. Just like a shrewd person can see right through a shady character, consumers who spend time with brands feel the inconsistencies between a brand and its package. And feel is the operative word. They may not see it, be able to articulate it, or even know it exists, but they know something is rotten in Denmark. Therefore it's less about having the right personality than being true to that personality. Consistency is where strength is built.

Knowing the personality requires clear definition before conception and then ongoing research as the brand matures. Because the brand is neither born nor will live in a vacuum, and because the world around it constantly changes, it will require additional knowledge and continued refinement. As a person ages and becomes more mature, you can see and feel the experience he or she has gained over the years. It's the same with a brand. Not with gray hair, but it gains the maturity to know when and how much to change to remain culturally relevant.

Brand personality can be defined by human personality techniques such as archetypes, profiles, Myers-Briggs, or a litany of others. Multiple definitions provide a variety of perspectives on the brand. Limiting it to one method is easier, but it risks leaving some aspect out. Once it has been defined, how much you push the personality depends on your place in the history of the category. If you're first to market, you have a greater obligation to identify the category and

set standards for how brands should behave in the newly formed category. This doesn't mean your personality has to come with a pocket protector, but it does lessen in importance relative to the other criteria. If you happen to be forty-fifth to market with a brand of water, you'll have to push beyond your comfort zone on personality, unless your water happens to cure cancer as well.

If your brand has been around for a while, understanding the difference between how you define the personality and how your audiences define it is valuable. The differences will reveal potential areas of inconsistency that should be considered as the brand and package evolve. Using the same methods or tests internally as you use externally will identify the gap and the potential for inconsistent brand messages.

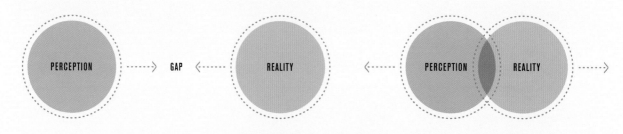

The more overlap between audience perceptions and the intended reality, the more consistency and strength in your brand. Brand personalities created and managed in such a way that creates distance from perception and reality will weaken the brand as audiences discover the inconsistencies. Strong brands are true to who they are.

SOURCE: CAPSULE

Cell phones have continued to advance
the technology while also realizing the
consumer desires a brand that reflects their
lifestyle. The ROKR phone package offers a
glimpse at the phone but more importantly,
a glimpse at the personality of the brand.

TURNER DUCKWORTH

"Kiss it, I dare ya. Go ahead, soul smack my slick, amphibian cricket hole. C'mon, tingle me. Just don't get your humanoid hopes up, pal, I ain't changin'. I like my slippery self just the way I am. Enough of my croakin', I've got stuff to Yank. Sure, I can impale flies all day long, but I'm after bigger thrills. Set out some fresh DVDs and CDs and let the Yankin' commence."

COPY TONE
Copy tone is very important when designing for a particular audience. For Yank, it's the antibranding Gen Yers.

TOUCHPOINTS
Adding personality to the expected creates a memorable touch point.

PACKAGING REQUIREMENTS
Personality does not need to be restricted by packaging requirements.

FEATURES AND BENEFITS
Instead of a typical list of features and benefits, a humorous pictograph system was used.

GET YOURSELF A PERSONALITY, PLEASE

Industries evolve, categories coalesce, and every package in a category starts to look the same. Going to a party where everyone looks, talks, sounds, and smells the same—whom do you want to hang out with? The one who isn't the same as all the rest? If you walk down store aisles today, you'll pick up on the personality attributes just by viewing and reading the packages. If you start to see common patterns, it's because many personalities follow others who have got there first.

Leaders take the chance of having personality attributes that are not commonly seen in the category, but this is risky. If an attribute isn't common in the category, might it be because it has already been tried and failed? Or has no one thought of it before? And could that really be the case? It depends on the radical nature of the category. For instance, when Healthy Choice frozen meals chose green as their primary color, they had to face the food category fear of that color. Green can be associated with rotting food, making it an uncommon color and a risk for the Healthy Choice brand. Bending or breaking with conventional wisdom is a hallmark of break-out brands, those brands that leave the others behind with their mouths gaping open and whispering, "How did they do that?"

Taking risks requires an understanding of what the real risks are in any situation. For instance, when something is uncomfortable, we chose to avoid and perhaps remove the discomfort instead of allowing ourselves to become comfortable or even analyzing our discomfort. This gut-wrenching emotional response can be a good contrast to the banal personalities likely to be shelved directly to the right and left of your brand. It can be a joy for the consumer to find something unique on the shelf, even if it was the result of a highly uncomfortable decision-making process. Translated, this means no emotional pain, no emotional gain.

Many times the biggest hurdle is getting your team (both client and design) to see the real risk. Making comparisons to other categories can be hugely instructive. By looking at other categories, you can zero in on products and packages that break away from their conventions—and draw valuable conclusions from the results. For instance, if you're in the food category, pick a category that's opposite (or least not similar) to food that you admire. In other words, looking at the peanut butter category isn't helpful if your product is honey (another food). Find something at some distance from your category— perfume, perhaps. As your team starts to review packaging, you can draw correlations to the categories you've studied, and you will find a team that's more comfortable with pushing personality boundaries.

As the breakfast cereal industry matured in the 1950s, cereal brands created characters like Tony the Tiger to infuse personality. In a world where impersonal technology is often the center of attention, seeing a bullfrog named B. Shizzle on the box cover for this DVD burner is an example of pushing personality.

CAPSULE

Criteria 4: Navigation

WHO MOVED MY PEANUT BUTTER, DAMN IT?

Walk into a retail environment and look around. Now, start counting the brands you can identify and those you cannot. If you begin to feel like you're counting stars in the sky, only less romantic, then you're getting it. Navigation in the age of pirates and treasure chests involved the challenge of crossing vast oceans. Today, consumers face the overwhelming task of navigating vast megastores stocked with brands and packages from all over the world. So if you want to help the pirates reach your treasure trove, you have to consider the importance of navigation when packaging a product and sending it out on the open market.

What happens when a consumer walks down the aisle? Exactly how does your package happily end up in his or her cart? By using design tools, consumers are given navigation clues to reach the destination you set out for them. There are navigation ele-ments that help move them through the category of options. And there are elements that get them to the exact SKU within your display of options.

Navigation, like identification, relies on visual cues like type, colors, patterns, words, shapes, and anything else that's visible on the package. Some parts of a package serve to connect it to the larger family of products, while other elements make the package utterly distinctive. The full effect of these elements can only be under-stood by looking at the category as a whole. This means either you have to have a keen ability to see something in context or the ability to create context in a digital environment. Either way, it's what matters when under-standing a package's contribution to navigation.

Limited navigation reduces the impact you can have on the category as your own personal billboard. It can also limit how someone shops your brand and the knowledge he or she gains about how connected your products are to one another. The extreme of no navigation is a missed opportunity at best and a drain on sales at worst.

Navigation can also work too hard and drown out the personality of indi-vidual products, flavors, or variations. This can leave the consumer feeling like an individual product is generic or lacking a unique touch. Imagine ice cream that identifies its rocky road flavor using only words and missing the tummy-tingling photo of peanuts, marshmallows, and chocolate. Not that enticing anymore, huh? Extremes are valuable teaching tools, but find-ing the right balance is what you need in practice. It's harder to teach and is left to be intuited and understood. Balance just feels right—and it feels right next to mint chocolate chip.

An illustrated approach to navigation, the Dr. Stuart's tea box gives shoppers many subtle clues to help navigate their way to the right choice. Colors may vary but Dr. Stuart's tea logo does not. Illustrations tell a more nuanced and metaphorical story for those willing to spend a little time with it.

PEARLFISHER

Dry Soda beverages are designed to match specific meals. These unique bottles contain similarly unique flavors like lemongrass, lavender, and kumquat. The package design sets the product apart from the cluttered beverage marketplace.

TURNSTYLE

Balancing what changes and what stays the same is key to packaging with high navigation. The Neutral line of products creates a simple navigational tool to follow by using icons and color. The consistency among all the packages gives Neutral a larger presence on the shelf, while facilitating navigation.

MUGGIE RAMADANI DESIGN STUDIO (MRDS)

With a dizzying array of options on the shelf today—especially when it comes to personal care products—sometimes it is all about a number. Find your way through a crowded field by choosing the product you desire and all you have to remember is one number. This illustrates navigation at the shelf made easy while still infusing personality into the brand.

BERGMAN ASSOCIATES

CONSUMERS MISBEHAVING: NAVIGATING THE AISLE

Consumers behave in apparently irrational and erratic ways. That is, until you spend time observing and analyzing why they do what they do. It may be highly emotional and it may not be what you want to see and hear, but it is their behavior. The package design can either contribute to navigation or just get in the way.

Spend some time in an aisle, any aisle. You'll start to see subtleties of consumer behavior. Record and question everything you see. For instance, you might find yourself in the nail care aisle watching women paint any flat surface of the display with nail enamel. What does this say about the package design? Perhaps the bottles are too easy to open, and women like to paint things. Or, more likely, the bottle doesn't show color accurately so these women use a dab of the color to see how it will look when they get home. It might also lead to an idea for paper nail samples to give these aisle artists a reason not to open the product. It may also lead to a bottle that represents color more accurately in the cap and to a product that gains an advantage at the shelf. Consumers' behavior may seem irra-

tional until ideas surface that address the behavior, and then the consumers are rational and valuable to the brand manager who achieves this greater understanding.

Decision-making modeling and behavior modeling goes far enough back that it should be on the tongue of any marketer with a degree today. Unfortunately, this is often not the case. They are simple tools used to map out consumer behavior and then to perform experiments to achieve the desired reaction. Perhaps in an effort to get someone to purchase your brand over another you spend zillions of dollars getting the consumer to recognize your brand name and be able to talk about it at parties. Then, what happens in the store? Can they remember?

Decision-making diagrams: consider them a framework but not the finite evidence of how consumers shop a category. The examples used are for nail care items, enamels, and implements; each offers a different perspective on how a shopper navigates each category. For those of you, 49 percent of the population, who may never purchase these items, you'll have to relate it to items you would buy.

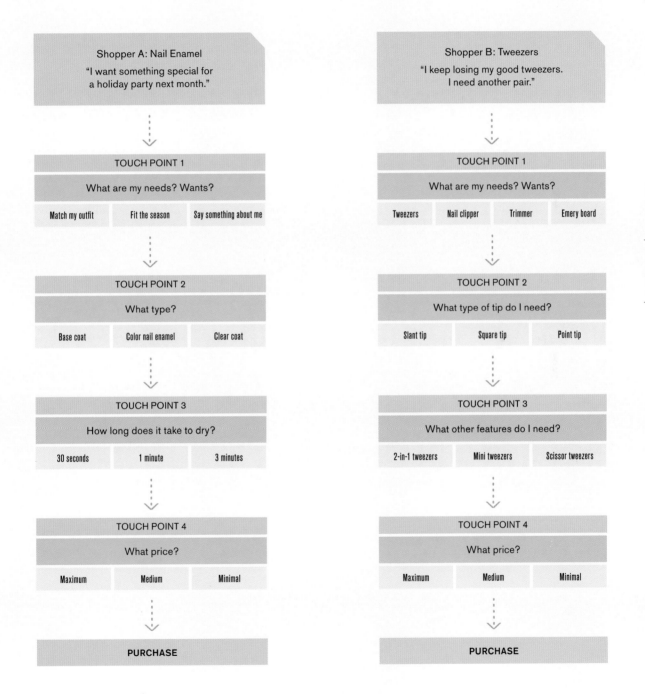

Shopper A: Nail Enamel

"I want something special for a holiday party next month."

TOUCH POINT 1

What are my needs? Wants?

| Match my outfit | Fit the season | Say something about me |

TOUCH POINT 2

What type?

| Base coat | Color nail enamel | Clear coat |

TOUCH POINT 3

How long does it take to dry?

| 30 seconds | 1 minute | 3 minutes |

TOUCH POINT 4

What price?

| Maximum | Medium | Minimal |

PURCHASE

Shopper B: Tweezers

"I keep losing my good tweezers. I need another pair."

TOUCH POINT 1

What are my needs? Wants?

| Tweezers | Nail clipper | Trimmer | Emery board |

TOUCH POINT 2

What type of tip do I need?

| Slant tip | Square tip | Point tip |

TOUCH POINT 3

What other features do I need?

| 2-in-1 tweezers | Mini tweezers | Scissor tweezers |

TOUCH POINT 4

What price?

| Maximum | Medium | Minimal |

PURCHASE

The tweezers are more of a task-driven purchase and therefore more focused on need (rational) and making the right decision faster. In contrast, the nail enamel decision, which is more driven by want (emotional), allows for exploration by the purchaser.

SOURCE: CAPSULE

THOUGHTFULLY CREATED FOR A MOMENT IN TIME. THE MOMENT A HAND REACHES OUT TO GRASP IT, PICK IT UP, TURN IT OVER, AND THEN PLACE IT IN A BASKET. DESIGN THE PERFECT PACKAGE, START WITH THE CONSUMER, AND WORK BACK TO A SPECIFIC MOMENT WHEN THE POWER OF DESIGN IS REALIZED.

Designing Packages

Design in the field of packaging is where the worlds of two-dimensional and three-dimensional design come together and shake hands. The typical package has a minimum of two sides and often many more. This combines the domains of product design and graphic design in an elegant merger that embraces the product itself.

Design is a discipline that is developed much like any craft, over a period of years under the right guidance, study, and tutelage. From materials to shapes and forms, to graphics on packages to openings and handles, there are many aspects of packaging design to understand. And just when everything seems crystal clear, an innovative new material or closure comes along.

As a package is often referred to as the salesperson on the shelf, the design process brings that person to life. And unless you want to bring another Frankenstein to life, a design team should aspire to create something people won't recoil from or reject out of hand. So the next question is, "Who would you like to have selling your product?"

This section covers how much the package contributes to the convenience and accessibility of the product it contains. It covers the three levels of packages—primary, secondary, and tertiary—and their purpose and potential. Then shape and structure come in to lend dimension and a unique form. Lastly, color, type, and art are the essential utensils of the design practitioner.

Design Green Thinkers

LIVING VERSUS ACTING SUSTAINABLY

Recently there have been several large elephants jumping up and down on the environmentally responsible bandwagon: Wal-Mart being the most notable. With its Sustainability Packaging Exposition, Wal-Mart introduced 3,000 product suppliers to 135 alternative packaging suppliers. Although this might bobble the heads of those who originally built the bandwagon, the effort is commendable. If you know any wagon builders, ask them this: "If there were a large corporation in the world you'd like to have singing the praises of the environmental movement, which one would it be? Who could make the greatest impact? What stores contain the most packages? Who could make it economical to be environmental?"

Although talking can get the ball rolling, the real action happens when the rubber hits the road. Or rather, when the bio-fiber, corn-based substance that feels like rubber but biodegrades in three hundred days hits the road.

We, as a design community, have all the tools at our disposal to make an impact with every package we design. Small steps make for little carbon footprints when it comes to an environmentally sound package.

Just inches of packaging material saved, or an extra moment spent considering the environmental impact from each part of the package, can yield profound results. The answer can't be, "It isn't important to our customers," because it will be. Nor can the answer be, "We think it's just a fad," because it's not. Books like *Cradle to Cradle*, *Natural Capitalism*, and others deliver great insight into how to think about the packages we create. In addition, both books hammer out the economic factors and the potential financial and social rewards for adopting responsible behaviors and a green business strategy.

Although consumer recycling certainly has great merit, it is not what stands to help the environment most. The "holy cow" impact will come from innovative new products and packages that use fewer raw materials, make it easier to reuse or recycle, and reduce the impact from point of origin to final destination. So what would be a good example? Stop shipping water. Or ship as little water as we possibly can. Studies have shown that homes in the civilized world already have equal or greater quality water on tap.

Need another example? Consider what *Cradle to Cradle* advocates: Keep biological innovations and industrial innovations separate when designing a package. Simple idea. When you have something that decomposes, make it easy to separate from the parts that need to be recycled. This means blending cardboards and unrecyclable plastics isn't good, but blending cardboard and bioplastics is. Keep it economically simple for the consumer. The impact is less and the reward greater.

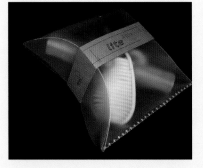

Many packages have secondary uses, but few see the value of having their branded package carry on in the life of your customer. The lite2go packaging that becomes the light with minimal assembly is a highly creative articulation of how to reuse.

KNOEND

SUSTAINABLE PACKAGING CONSIDERATIONS

••• Beneficial, safe, and healthy for individuals and communities throughout its life cycle

••• Meets market criteria for performance and cost

••• Sourced, manufactured, transported, and recycled using renewable energy

••• Maximizes the use of renewable or recycled source materials

••• Manufactured using clean production technologies and best practices

••• Made from materials that are healthy in all probable end-of-life scenarios

••• Physically designed to optimize materials and energy

••• Can be effectively recovered and utilized in biological and/or industrial *Cradle to Cradle* cycles

website: www.sustainablepackaging.org

PLANNING | **CREATING** | IMPLEMENTING

DESIGN MATTERS // PACKAGING 01

Sustainable Design Behaviors

"IF ONLY" IS BOLOGNA

We've all heard phrases that start with "If only" followed by some idealistic statement about saving the world with the flip of a light switch or the flush of a toilet. Idealism has its place, but if you want change, make it economic. Take a dollar from my pocket tomorrow and I'll turn off the lights early tonight. Oil prices go up and suddenly the environmental movement, sustainability, energy independence, and other related topics are part of virtually everyone's daily coffee conversation.

The same applies to packaging: Real change will happen when it makes solid economic sense. And it will make economic sense, unless it's trendy. Trends come and go. Hollywood likes trendy; environmental activists do not. If protecting the big blue marble we all live on becomes merely trendy, we're all in big trouble. Jumping out of your stretch SUV at an awards show and saying "I buy offsets" to the first reporter who asks a question should not, repeat, not be the standard behavior. Get your own behaviors in order first before buying offsets and bragging to your red

carpet fans. And for starters, make it a stretch hybrid.

But what are we doing about the box? Where will the package be when it stops moving or nears the end of its useful life? Will it need to be burned or buried to hide it from our fussy suburban eyes? Or will it need to be deconstructed in order to reintroduce each separate piece into a recycling program? Will it be used to fuel our homes? Could it be planted in the ground to grow a flower? These are the questions that Bill McDonough, author of *Cradle to Cradle*, posed to many corporate design teams long before it became hot to say, "Hi, I'm carbon neutral, how are you?" McDonough's efforts may not have led the consumer products environmental movement, but they have been recognized as important cogs in the system of sustainable design.

If your first thought is to use recycled materials when considering an environmentally responsible design, then you need to get current on your considerations because there are so many more factors at work.

Which is the more disposable cutlery, wood or plastic? If you choose wood, aren't you then cutting down the trees we hug? Not if they've fallen down already or if the wood is leftover from other sources. And what if we used wooden cutlery more than once because it is more durable and doesn't have the social stigma of hand-washed plastic forks? Thoughtful change leads to sustainable designs for Aspenware/Wun cutlery.

BLOK DESIGN

WASTE CREATION AND WHERE IT GOES

Country	Municipal Waste Per Capita	Percent Recycled	Percent Incinerated	Percent Land-filled
Austria	480k	38	14	48
Belgium	470k	14	31	55
Canada	630k	19	6	75
Czech Republic	230k	-	-	99
Denmark	530k	23	54	22
Finland	410k	33	2	65
Germany	400k	29	17	51
Greece	310k	7	-	93
Hungary	420k	-	7	93
Iceland	560k	14	17	69
Ireland	430k	8	-	92
Italy	470k	-	6	94
Japan	400k	4	69	27
Korea	390k	24	4	72
Luxembourg	530k	28	43	28
Mexico	330k	1	-	99
The Netherlands	580k	38	27	35
Norway	620k	15	16	69
Poland	290k	2	-	98
Portugal	350k	12	-	88
Spain	370k	12	4	83
Sweden	440k	19	42	39
Switzerland	610k	40	46	14
Turkey	590k	2	2	81
UK	490k	7	9	83
USA	720k	27	16	57

Source: Municipal Waste in OECD Countries (mid 1990s), ARUP Drivers of Change 2006 and AAAS Atlas

Figures based on available data

Waste not, want not. As the world breeds more consumption societies, waste needs to find its proper place in the economic cycle. These statistics represent current behaviors that will obviously not be sustainable behaviors.

Primary, Secondary, Tertiary

ONE, TWO, THREE; NOT IN THAT ORDER

The six-pack of bottles (primary) with a simple handled, collapsible package (secondary) and the insulated box that keeps your product cool and fresh while in transport (tertiary). These three layers of packages all contribute something important to the process of delivering a product from manufacturer to consumer.

Ever take a peek behind those plastic flaps protecting the backroom doorway at your local grocery store? Or better yet, did you ever have a job restocking shelves at a neighborhood convenience store? Remember all the boxes? Tertiary packages, also known as transport packaging, offer protection, transport, and some navigation for the participants in the channel. Because consumers rarely see the tertiary package, the logical result is a box with little or no brand messaging. But change is near as big box retailers have pallets of product displayed above or below the primary merchandise. Tertiary packaging's original and chief role was defined mainly by efficiencies obtained through manufacturing, packing, palletizing, shipping, storing, and unpacking. Today, tertiary packaging needs to keep its eye on function while looking toward a not-so-distant future with an emphasis on what it can do when it is sitting in bulk on a pallet.

Try carrying six bottles of beer from the liquor store shelf to your home, or better yet twenty-four bottles of water. Secondary packaging is the blending point between the function-driven tertiary packaging and the more brand-driven primary packaging. Secondary packaging often serves an important role in the display of a product on the shelf with such items as trays, display packs, and shipping packers. This means the secondary package has to be given nearly as much consideration as the primary package. Part of the consideration is based on what brand personality attributes should be conveyed on the secondary versus the primary package. Other considerations may include how the secondary package will stack, how it will contain the product while offering access, and how retailers will dispose of it. When the secondary package is successful, it balances function over form while offering a brand personality complement to the primary package.

As the anchor in a relay race from manufacturer to consumer, the primary package gets the attention and the rewards that come with being closest to the consumer. The primary package—i.e., the bottle that sits on your table or the can of soup in your pantry—is where most brands put their greatest investment and attention.

With this attention comes a storehouse of science and research surrounding what a primary package should accomplish. In the end, the primary package has the lead on a consumer relationship and needs to be designed to represent that leadership position in the array of packaging being leveraged. It needs to find that perfect balance of form and function and it must work hard in every context in which it will live.

Important, yes; overemphasized, maybe. With all the current changes in retailing, the primary package sometimes takes on the role as the only face of the brand, emphasis on only. This means that everything a consumer knows of the brand originates from the approximately six panels on the package. If this is true, the first issue is the missed opportunity to build a stronger relationship between the brand and a loyal consumer. The second issue is the consumer's desire to seek out knowledge of brands in their life—i.e., does the brand continue to live past the package? Be careful, because what they may find is not always good. For example, take an environmentally conscious brand with a primary package designed with every consideration for sustainability. What happens when the company's CEO is found acting environmentally irresponsible or a tertiary package is designed with little or no consideration for sustainable practices? The primary package definition should be given primary responsibility for leadership, but it should not take all the resources and attention away from the rest of the brand assets.

PRIMARY

SECONDARY

U'LUVKA VODKA

FRIENDSHIP LOVE & PLEASURE

TERTIARY

From the moment it leaves its home, this brand of vodka is packaged in a stylish custom bottle (primary), which goes inside a tasteful paperboard box (secondary), and then gets shipped inside an elegantly designed corrugated cardboard box (tertiary). All three pieces of a premium vodka packaging experience done right.

ALOOF DESIGN

Convenience and Access

THE MASTER CHURCH KEY

Completely contained, safety sealed, protected, air tight, and ready to handle almost any shipping hazard. Now, how do we get this thing open? Access is all about making the product available when the consumer needs it, at the exact right moment. More easily sought after than accomplished.

Being able to open a bottle of aspirin while battling a searing headache can be a challenge. But that same package can't be accessible to chubby toddler fingers. The bottom line is that consumers, retailers, and the environment pay the price to restrict access while the product lives at the store. Once it leaves the store, the rest of us have to deal with

the unpleasant task of extracting our new music CD, camping gadget, or pediatric thermometer. Access for the right person at the right time is one of many design challenges.

There's a frontier of possibilities when it comes to ideas that can be designed to give easy access to the right person. As a prototypical example, the blister lock provides a new way to look at the safety seal of a package.

Where will your package make itself useful? What tools will surround it and what purpose will they serve? These questions get to the context of use and create an ability to see the larger, slightly pixilated picture of the

consumer situation. The design can then create a new value for the consumer by increasing the convenience of the product while adding positive attributes to the brand.

Due to the ever-increasing frantic pace of life for most people—go there, find this, do that, and get back as soon as possible—packages need to fit in and make a contribution. By understanding how your package melds with consumers' lives and integrates convenience, the package can contribute. Closures and convenience factors can be large contributors to this growing consumer demand.

Making something convenient for parents but inaccessible to children is an elegant balance. Add to it a refill aspect and this design's achievement is impressive.

CHARGE INDUSTRIAL DESIGN

Convenience and access are fundamental. Each makes a sizeable contribution to product value by helping the consumer save time and effort, thereby streamlining some aspect of their daily lives.

Packaging slips into our lives and often makes a quiet impact on how we perceive the brand. The Carlo Giovani tea box packages entertain both adults and children and have proven to be a great example of the "packaging-as-toy" idea.
CARLO GIOVANI

Shape and Structure

THE SEXY NUCLEAR PHYSICIST

If you were blindfolded and someone put five similar products in front of you, could you pick out your brand of choice? The next time you're consuming a product right from the package, close your eyes and ask, "What do I feel?" Do you feel the shape, texture, and general structure of the package? Is it unique to this brand? Shape and structure can be made simple; put the product in a box that's strong enough to handle moderate damage during transport and you're done. Or, it can be more complex, innovative, and satisfying.

The shape of a package says something about a brand that graphics, colors, and typography cannot. At a minimum, it tells the consumer that someone spent time considering the shape of the package to make it unique and pleasing. Shape combines the sense of touch and sight to create a more lasting bond. Touch is a powerful sense, and yet it gets minimal consideration when it comes to managing brands. So, when a brand manager considers touch in package shape or texture, it earns an additional bit of attention from consumers. Think about the feel of a Coke bottle or the paper used

to wrap your favorite guilty pleasure, that dark chocolate bar hiding in the back of the freezer. Consider the items in your life that you touch and what the sense of touch communicates to you. With the sense of touch, accompanied by sight, the shape of a package can identify your brand on the shelf and offer the essential point of consistency in the brand's life.

Rapid prototyping technology advancements have given packaging designers the gift of seeing their work come to life in three-dimensional form. High-tech printers can build a model of your package design in a

matter of minutes by printing a layer of glue and then a layer of cornstarch. After hundreds of layers of each, the result is an off-white shape that can give everyone on the team a realistic feel for the final package shape and form. Then, take this prototype into consumer testing and you've got another level of knowledge that costs much less than it did a decade ago.

Structure, although most often considered for the purposes of protection and mere functional benefits, has other important attributes. The structure of a package determines its

The Vodafone brand owns the red quotation mark; this custom package design gives the quote dimension. The quote packages a phone card and more importantly shows us how a valuable brand asset can come to life in a package design.

MILK LTD

What does wealth feel like in your hand? If rose nectar happens to be your preferred liquid, this bottle would answer the question. Sence is a rare European rose nectar that originates from a harvested rose blossom. The package is designed to evoke an experience suggesting the opulence of the flower itself.

ADAM TIHANY/TIHANY DESIGN

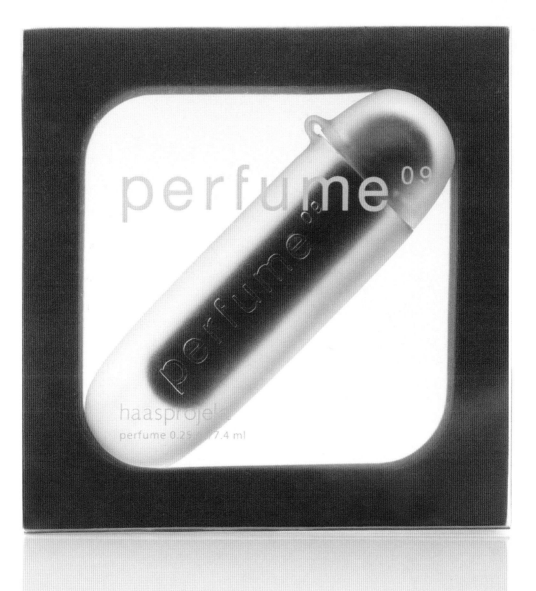

This package conveys the simple elegance of a perfume capsule within a stunning red box. Packaged to deliver an experience to the shopper with a desire for this perfume, it not only creates a sexy, alluring shape; it also merchandises nicely.

FUSEPROJECT

presence on the shelf but it also can determine how it fits into the hands of consumers. Structure in packaging design is best equated to building bridges, roads, and strong buildings. If the package doesn't have the proper structure, it doesn't stand a chance when faced with a forklift operator having a bad day. The trials and tribulations a package faces as it travels to market can be pleasant one day and terrifying the next. This is where structural thinking can help keep the product protected, contained, and uncontaminated during its journey.

Structure is becoming increasingly significant as we enter the current phase of the sustainable design movement. As new materials become available, they need to be structurally capable of performing at the same, if not higher, level as their predecessors. As the shape and form of packages change for the sake of sustainable design and greater efficiencies, the structure must be considered. With all the evolutions in materials, manufacturing methods, and sustainable design methods, packaging structure offers a great opportunity for design but also demands great responsibility to keep our standards at the highest level.

Respect must be paid to those who understand and consider shape and structure in the design process. And, for those who do not, the folly of a clumsy, poorly engineered and embarrassing package design looms on their horizon.

Shape and structure work together to form the foundation of a successful package design.

Lower Tibet offers the world a gift of tranquil energy from the goji berry harvested for this juice. The package is as magical as the liquid it contains, looking first like art and then like a unique bottle of juice.
GLOJI, INC.

Many package shapes are unique enough to be recognized by their silhouette alone. Consider what owning a shape can do to prevent competitors from copying your product offering.

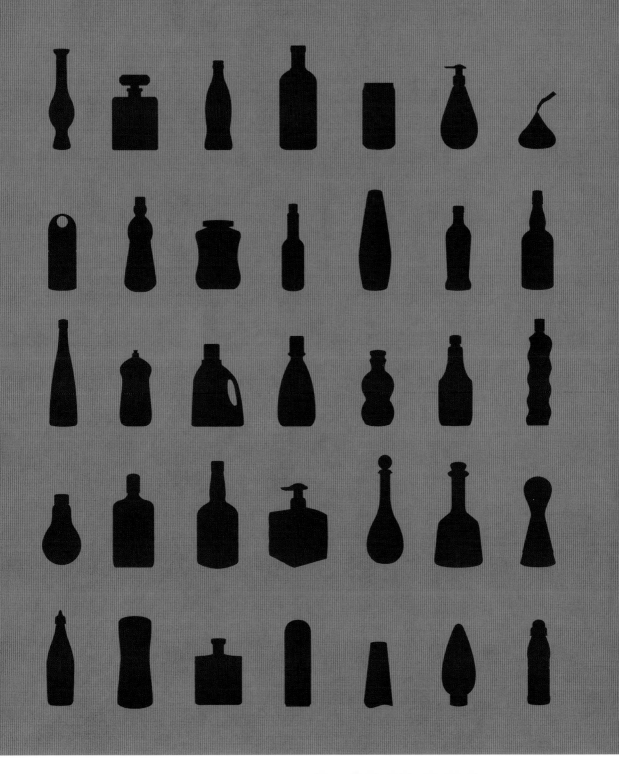

Color, Type, and Art

THREE ROADS CONVERGE IN THE WOODS

Designing a package today is made to look easy. Get a flat screen monitor, a Mac tower, some Adobe software, buy a library of typefaces and photography, teach yourself the basics, and you're on the road. Right? Some might say, "It's easier than flipping burgers." But then you start to make decisions. This typeface versus that one, red versus blue, this photograph versus that illustration. Where does it lead? There is a reason why design professionals apprentice for a period of time and a reason why they're constantly seeking greater knowledge and applying it to their work. Design isn't about pulling your stool up to the magical technology tap and adding three parts color theory, one part typeface, and two parts imagery.

Behind all three of these legs—color, type, and art—are theories, cultural norms, practices, and a host of other factors to consider. In color, the science of how our eyes see overlaps with color theory, which is connected more closely with art than actual science. Leave your country of residence and ask someone the meaning of a certain color. White is always an interesting choice as Western cultures see sterile and clean, purity and innocence, while many Eastern cultures see death and mourning. Then we have to travel down the road of color harmony to find which colors work well together and what they say together. This can seem entirely too complicated when all you want is a new package design. As programmers read code and see an application, designers read colors and see a contextual result. They design color combinations to be trademarked by brand owners. They use color to break out of category conventions or fit into them. And all the while they use it to convey the brand personality, leveraging all the emotion wrapped up in colors.

When it comes to type, with serifs and sans serifs, the number of options seems staggering. Are there thousands, hundreds of thousands? And what does a certain serif communicate and how does it read from three different distances? What typeface complements the serif but offers a smart contrast on the package? Type is a fertile area for making horrific mistakes on a package. For example, using a script typeface on something that needs to be legible from a few feet away is ill advised. At least we have regulations for ingredients and nutritional facts. A common mistake is using more than three—and what sometimes seems like more than ten—different typefaces

Color is often used to convey varieties and flavors of a product line. This package design uses color without hitting the shopper over the head with primary colors. The result is a highly functional package with a personality worth getting to know.

HORNALL ANDERSON DESIGN WORKS

on a single package design. If each typeface has a personality, doesn't the ten-typeface package suggest a multiple personality disorder? Type is core to the hierarchy of information, using bold to get attention, italics for product benefits, and all caps for functional information. But don't let the simplicity of type fool you. Dig deep into the nuances of type, and you may find yourself respecting it more and even becoming a type addict. Don't worry, there's a nine-step program available at your local art store, not that we recommend it.

Art isn't just for artists anymore. Here, art can mean photography and illustration, not just Monet. Art delivers a message and tells part of the brand story. If you know the brand story, you can focus your efforts around certain art forms that work better than others. Art conveys a feeling and like everything else, it can be interpreted and understood. It can range from fine art to illustration to photography. Each piece is created to communicate some form of meaning—attaching that meaning to the brand is what needs to be carefully thought out. Just picking art because you like it may give you a sense of inner joy but may do nothing for the consumer or the marketer of the product. Art can be debated just like any other part of the package: If you can defend it both rationally and emotionally, then your choice is probably appropriate.

As the package starts to come together, you've delved into type, art, and color, and what have you found? Consistency. The word that has all three of these parameters joined together like an old-fashioned ménage à trois. The goal is to be consistent with an unshakable understanding of what the brand means to the consumer who buys it. Introduce a color that doesn't make sense and you've got a mess on your hands. Do it right and there's reason to celebrate; do it wrong and the party's over.

The interaction between the color of the product and the package can be easily overlooked. But when it is planned for, the result can be amazing and amusing. The Jubes candy line uses contrasting colors to engage and entertain.

KINETIC SINGAPORE

How do fashionistas throw a party? Just like the rest of us, but with a lot more flair. Where do you find flair? Right here, inside this package of cocktails by Jenn. Using color-coding and iconography, the packaging is a welcome accessory at any party.

MICHAEL OSBORNE DESIGN

Il Fornaio olive oil is another nugget from Australia to be shared with the world. Referred to as a vessel, this package draws from all the visual and tactile cues of Tuscany, Italy.

HOYNE DESIGN

Engineering and Testing

NO PACKAGE IS AN ISLAND

Package design is integral to the entire manufacturing process that starts with creating a product and ends with delivery to the consumer. How the package fits into that manufacturing process is one part of the package engineering discipline. The other parts include food safety, tamper-evident closures, chemical interactions, cushioning, regulations, RFID, distribution, and testing for each. Some of these disciplines are covered by the packaging engineer; while other aspects fall under operations or quality control. Either way, they are essential to help your beautiful package become smarter. For you to become smarter, we touch on a few of the subjects, leaving you with the desire to find more through other sources.

Shelf stability doesn't refer to whether your package will fall on a small child, but rather, will the contents remain the same over time. Put another way, how long will it take to see chunks in your milk? Unfortunately it's not that simple, as the process to determine shelf stability is highly complex and factors in many variables. Because many consumable products will change properties and efficacy as they get exposed to air and light, their shelf stability is a critical timeline for the manufacturer and retailer. This shouldn't be confused with the "Born on" or "Enjoy by" date you find on your favorite malt beverage. This is the science behind those claims and much more essential to the safety and viability of the product.

Engineering a package requires the right education combined with experience to get a package to work the way it was intended. It ranges from material tests to make sure it can handle all climate conditions to drop tests to make sure it will handle the average store clerk. The engineer of a package has many tools and resources, but the real talent is putting them to use creatively to find an optimal solution. This may mean numerous prototypes, molds, and mockups. It may also mean some hardcore predictive mathematics in order to insure that the package being built will live up to the promises we attach to it. And, of course, it needs to make it to the shelf.

Distribution or logistics is the science behind getting something specific to a specific location at a specific time in the most specific and efficient manner possible. Logistics is also the backbone and the intelligence supporting the largest retailer in the world, Wal-Mart. The relationship between packaging design and logistics can be challenging. If you're not careful, logistical requirements will work against what is most attractive about the original package design. Logistics can also be the largest constraining factor when it comes to

Does the juice market need another option? If you have less time in your day than disposable income to stay healthy, then perhaps there is a place for Wild Bunch & Co. This bottle has a simple resealing closure to extend the freshness of this organic juice.
SEED CREATIVE

creative solutions that fall outside the standard "box" design. This doesn't mean combating logistics with verbal abuse—it means learning all that you can about how your package fits into the logistics process. And then translating your learning into thoughtfully designed answers to logistics challenges.

Cushioning refers to how well your package protects the product inside from vibration and shock. Vibration comes from the perpetual movement a package endures on its way to market. Shock comes from the six-foot (1.8 m) drop by a lanky and clumsy warehouse employee. Although these are obvious, others include the impact from static electricity, temperature, and moisture. The engineering analysis turns to labor rates and manufacturing and material costs to arrive at a final outcome. In most cases it will include an expected damage rate because absolute protection is both cost prohibitive and presents a diminishing rate of return. In other words, it costs more to protect products from every possible injury than it does to lose an estimated number of units.

You can test almost anything to reach a reasonable level of confidence. The disciplines discussed previously have methods to ensure the highest level of confidence in each of the aspects. Testing can involve a focus group watching adults as they struggle to open a new child safety top on a pill bottle. More complex methods of drop testing, chemical interaction, and others lead to greater understanding of how the packaging will interact with the product inside or the environment outside. The broader objective of any testing is to reduce risk when taking a package to market.

Testing should increase or decrease confidence in one or more aspects of your package design. This doesn't have to destroy what's good about the package if the results are taken as a jumping-off point to make improvements or create a wholly new package design. Ignore the findings from testing and you may find yourself in a tight spot when the product hits the shelves and the results are more than disappointing. Understand the methods, embrace the results, and you may find new territory your design team has yet to explore.

In dangerous situations, we look to engineering to keep us safe. This package for LP gas is 50 percent lighter because it uses a polyethylene composition. The design team, however, didn't rely on material alone. They included a clean, elegant design with comfortable handles for efficient lifting. Now all men have something worthy of sitting beside our coveted gas grills.

BRANDIA CENTRAL

IMPLEM

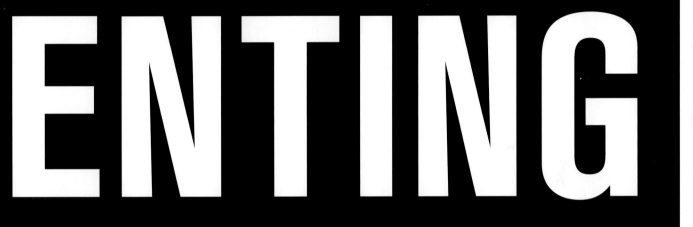

ENTING

"THERE ARE TWO KINDS OF PEOPLE, THOSE WHO FINISH WHAT THEY START AND SO ON." — ROBERT BYRNE

THE ARMANI SUIT WITH A BLACK TIE, THE PLATE MAIL ENGLISH ARMOR, AND THE LEATHER CHAPS WITH A TEN-GALLON HAT. FROM LEATHER TO STEEL TO THREADS, FROM TOP TO BOTTOM AND SIDE-TO-SIDE, EACH PACKAGES AN IMAGE IN YOUR MIND.

Types, Materials, and Faces

From stock types of packages such as clamshells, bottles, cans, flexible bags, boxes, and tubes to an unimaginable number of unique types and hybrids, the possibilities reach farther than most people can imagine. Types of packages are constrained only by the current collective imagination of the global creative community.

A similar idea applies to materials used to leverage packaging design. Each material on its own has attributes such as weight, structure, strength, permeability, texture, colors, and many other aspects that either contribute to or contrast with the product being packaged.

Category conventions, manufacturability, and basic economics will drive much of the material decisions. This is the reason we seldom, if ever, see bread packaged in aluminum or peanut butter in polymer bags. The real contribution packaging materials can make is in the creative use of materials in between these examples. When a vodka bottle needs to feel just right in the hands of a bartender, or the rubber on the base creates the feeling of the super-premium vodka Effen.

The multitude of faces a package contains offers the opportunity to tell a dimensional story about the brand. Just following conventions would likely lead to the same information on the back of a package organized in much the same way. This might be interesting to a socialist engineer, but the rest of the world craves variety. The other faces of a package set a stage for showcasing the brand's ability to prove its uniqueness.

Package Types

PLEASE DON'T TYPECAST MY PACKAGE

Carton, box, tube, bottle, can, bag, clamshell, blister, label, and hybrids—walk around a superstore and packaging types start to categorize themselves. Walk a little further and you start to notice patterns in each aisle or category. And then just a bit further until you start seeing the rogue products, those that are packaged in a manner entirely different than the existing category patterns. And then there are those that combine types of packages to create new concepts of how a package type should function.

Bear Naked granola cereals in stand-up resealable bags. Frozen orange juice in a rectangular jug that you refrigerate for a few hours before use. Honey that comes in a beehive-shaped plastic bottle from Granja San Francisco of Barcelona, Spain.

Packages are in every crevice of our lives and can either complicate or simplify our lives.

Gourmet Garden parsley-herb blend in a plastic tube. All examples of packages that take an unconventional approach to their package type and offer a glimpse into how a new product can set itself apart on the shelf.

Now step into someone's home and you can see a package doing a hard day's work. Type of package can be heavily influenced by the context of use. If your package shows up on a pantry shelf and requires users to continually reseal the bag inside the box, they'll most likely look elsewhere for a similar product. Studies have shown that a vast majority of consumers are none too organized. We strive to be more organized but have limits on time, resources, and energy that keep us from reaching organization utopia.

Package types offer a variety of options that should be considered for the impact in the manufacturing line, distribution channel, retail environment, and finally, inside the consumption context.

*Naked stock packages. There are many stock options
available from a variety of packaging sources. This
selection came from Comp24: www.comp24.com.
Walk around your local retailer and you'll find many
more examples of stock packages to source.*

CAPSULE

Material Options

YES, MADONNA, WE DO LIVE IN A MATERIAL WORLD

Paper, plastic, glass, leather, fake fur, foam, cork, metal, wood, textiles, rubber, composites, and new materials are being developed every day. The possibilities are endless, intriguing, and sometimes a little scary.

What does it feel like to pick up a small wooden box? What is the message associated with each of the materials you use? If the medium is vital to conveying the message, paraphrasing from our studious Marshall McLuhan, the material used impacts your message. An area where packaging designers dive deep into the

abyss of possibilities is material, as it is derived from many sources, locations, and manufacturers.

Materials are most commonly paired with certain package types: Corrugated fiberboard boxes, glass bottles, and aluminum cans are classic examples. This is where the design mind can start reformulating to have corrugated plastic boxes, aluminum bottles, or even plastic cans. Start blending materials and creating hybrid combinations, and you may find some interesting results.

Ever have the moment when something makes you say, "I wish I'd thought of that"? TwentyFour Wine has a rubber band label, a unique material that keeps the bottle from slipping in your hand. Yeah, me too.

STUDIOBENBEN

Hugo Boss: Men's Skin product line is designed to feel like a German engineered automobile, something most men can't resist. Although the materials give it a sleek look, the full experience waits until it's in the hands of the consumer.

WEBB SCARLETT DEVLAM

Cabo Uno was made famous by the former Van Halen front man Sammy Hagar. Wood, leather, lead-free crystal, and one amazing liquid. Combined you can find it for $250 (£127). Materials blended like this add up to a genuinely unique experience.

MEAT AND POTATOES, INC.

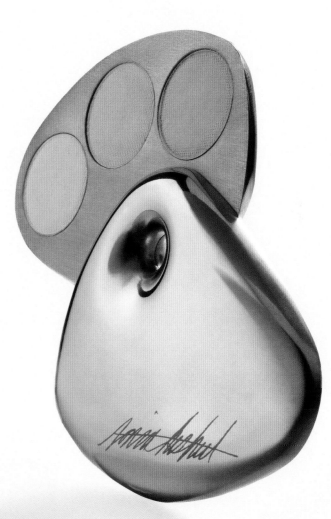

Everyday materials in unexpected contexts can provide a unique experience. This Sonia Kashuk design for fragrance packaging includes two products: a solid compact and a liquid bottle. The result is a product you can personalize to your individual preference. The bottle, if it can be called such, is made from aluminum to create a tactile sensation.

HARRY ALLEN & ASSOCIATES

MATERIAL OPTIONS

Within each of the aforementioned categories (glass, plastic, etc) there are many permutations and variations. The variations offer details like textured or heat-sensitive plastics or nonslip rubber or extra sticky rubber. Each detail can offer another element to build on the experience of the product and the package.

Keeping up on new materials can be done online (www.materialconnexion.com) or through other material sources in industrial design circles. Get samples, keep them around the office, and buy things you find that incorporate creative materials. Organize the materials by weight, feel, cost, and any other parameter that is important to your design process. You'll be surprised how oftentimes just having a unusual material nearby will lead to its being used in a package design.

KU-GREEN PACKAGING
Molded fiber packaging that uses tapioca starch. This patented composition incorporates nominally 90 percent cassava starch, 10 percent plant fibers, and a small amount of food-grade additives. As it is temporary in design, it's a great option for single-use food packaging, home delivery meals, outdoor food fairs, fast food restaurants, or catering packages.

BARK CLOTH
Moldable flexible surfaces manufactured from tree bark. Taken from Ugandan ficus trees, the material is transformed by mechanical deformation into a soft, flexible textile (like sheets) that has mechanical strength and good abrasion resistance. A beautiful and decorative accent material for luxury products of many forms.

NATURAL PLASTIC BY METABOLIX
Polyhydroxyalkanoate is the name for polymers that are produced from natural resources using a process of fermentation from natural sugars and oils. A possible replacement for many plastics used in injection-molded plastics and thermoforming situations. In other words, a more disposable package for disposable packages.

BIOXO BY CASCADE
Degradable polystyrene foam-molded parts designed to degrade in three years versus the hundred years for traditional polystyrene. Spend some time atop your local landfill and consider what it would be like if we had this thirty years ago. Possible uses include anything you've packaged with polystyrene in the past and any products where three years isn't an issue.

MEDGUARD BY COOLEY GROUP

Highly durable, woven or felted polyester is an alternative to PVC that can be incinerated without emitting toxic fumes. Useful for packages you know have or will have a high likelihood of being incinerated or used as fuel for someone's fire.

DEGRADABLE PLASTICS BY D2W

Imaging a time delay on the degrading of the plastic bag designed for a bread company. How about eighteen months? The best part is that these polyethylene and polypropylene plastics don't need special conditions; just add air. The range of possible applications is endless—limited only by our collective imagination.

BIO PDO BY PIONEER AND TATE & LYLE

Fossil fuels are renewable; it just takes a mere hundred-plus years to produce more. Corn-based polymers have the benefit of less than one year to renew. Bio PDO is a polymer that uses 40 percent less energy to produce and reduces greenhouse gas emissions by 20 percent. Applications are as vast as the number of packages that use plastics.

EARTHSHELL

Food-safe, biodegradable foam laminate packaging materials. Created by combining potato starch, corn, limestone, and a bit of recycled fiber, which is then heat-pressed into shape. Immediate applications include disposable meals and fast food; going forward, applications expand to many food categories.

CEREPLAST

This blended polyactic acid plastic comes from a variety of biodegradable ingredients that keep the cost low and the versatility high. There are currently ten resin formulas that are optimized for injection molding, blow molding, thermoforming, and extrusion. This is an amazing material option for disposable and other packages in need of a balance between protection and environmental responsibility.

ABS / POM / PP BY KARELINE OF SWEDEN

All injection moldable resins that contain a large portion of natural fibers. Each has unique properties and applications. For instance, the polystyrene-based composites have a lovely surface quality that would add interesting personality to jewelry, cosmetics, or other beauty products.

GARDEN GREETINGS BY BOTANICAL PAPERWORKS

Looking to plant your package in consumers' minds and their backyards? Botanical Paperworks has paper products with embedded seeds. A number of socially responsible products—and certainly children's products—could benefit from this feel-good, earth-friendly feature.

INNOVIA FILMS

Heat sealable and biodegradable can be a tough marriage. Innovia Films pull it off by using 95 to 100 percent regenerated wood pulp. Biodegradable and worthy of your backyard compost heap, this material is terrific for food, household items, and personal care products.

SHEEP POO PAPER BY CREATIVE PAPER WALES

Not to be confused with paper made from elephant dung or reindeer droppings, this is Sheep Poo Paper from Wales, where they know their sheep. Forget your first worry: the odor has been eliminated without using intense chemicals. Sheep Poo Fiber from sheep with plenty of fiber is a great material for anything with a sense of humor and any clothing made from wool.

TERRASKIN

Drawing on the chemistry of eggshell material, this polymer film has the unique ability to slowly decompose into sand when exposed to sunlight. The material is microwavable, recyclable, and is FDA approved for fatty or dry food items. Obvious applications include any number of food items and perhaps any number of items that trace their origins to salt or calcium carbonate.

Front, Sides, Bottom, Top, and Back

SIX FACES, ONE PERSONALITY

Consider the salesperson metaphor again when looking at the faces on a package and the hierarchy of information on each. If it all looks exactly the same, then ask if you've just created the shallowest salesperson on the team. Procter & Gamble calls it the first moment of truth when the consumer picks up the package. Compare it to your initial handshake with the individual selling you a Mercedes. What does the first moment feel like when a consumer picks up your package? Does it feel heavy or light, soft or hard, flexible or rigid, sticky or slippery?

Then as you walk around the sales lot looking at gorgeous cars, what do you notice? Is the salesperson wearing ratty old sneakers under his suit? What does that mean? Does this individual smell like tanning beds? You know that smell. When the consumer turns your package over to one side,

the consistency in personality should be there, literally and visually. Does the back of the package communicate truths about the brand? If the consumer gets to the bottom of the package, will he or she find dirt or scuffs on it? Does it matter? Did your last Mercedes salesperson have mud on his shoes?

As consumers become more marketing savvy, they not only filter more, but they also know when something is being "sold" to them, even when it comes to package design. Considering this modern consumer, the package front must do its best to set the first sale and then be consistent for any repeat purchases. The other faces of the package must offer a look inside the brand, so the consumer can sense the truth of the brand from how it's designed to how the information is organized on each panel.

When designing a package, consider context and creatively discover ways the package can insert itself into the situation or conversation. Consider method home's dish soap package: It takes package design to the level of a piece of art that might not be as readily shoved beneath the sink.

The other faces often offer great opportunities for design because the consumer must commit to the package by holding it in order to spend time looking at the other faces. In other words, once you've got them engaged, how are you going to keep them connected? If the front of the package works to entice a consumer to pick it up, the rest of the package needs to get it into the cart.

Regulations keep honest brands honest and keep dishonest brands on the run. Regulations are inherently not fun but always necessary.

CAPSULE

Standards and guidelines keep this part of a package design consistent across many product categories. Infusing a bit of brand personality requires a delicate touch.

TURNSTYLE

Barcode systems are nearly ubiquitous in nature, but with a bit of creativity and patience, the brand personality can be reflected in this part of the package.

CAPSULE

FUNNEL: ERIC KASS: UTILITARIAN + COMMERCIAL
+ FINE: ART

FEATURES, BENEFITS, EMOTIONAL REWARDS

▶ Now that the shopper has picked up the package, how does your story continue? How do the features, benefits, and emotional rewards come to life on the package? This is where you go more in depth into why consumers should place the package in their basket, and where the body of your brand story comes to life and concludes with emotional and rational reasons to make the purchase.

MANDATORY ELEMENTS

▶ Depending on the category, country, region, or brand, mandatory elements vary. In the U.S. market, children's toys, food, alcohol, and electronics are subject to regulations meant to protect the consumer. The best place to start is with existing packages. Then regional, national, and international governmental authorities offer websites with exhaustive information on guidelines, regulations, and specific requirements.

INGREDIENTS AND INSTRUCTIONS

▶ When you can't see everything that's inside a particular product, it's good to know what you're buying. Inventory lists, checklists, and other specifics are comforting to anyone who may not fully understand the contents. The same goes for instructions: they can promote a clear benefit of one brand over another through simple installation and use instructions.

Weights, Measures, and Barcodes

STAND UP FOR STANDARDS

Locate something that requires standards and boundaries, and at a close distance you'll find those who bend the rules. Sure, bending is good, but knowing when you've broken them is better. The weights, measures, and barcodes required on a package are there for a legitimate and valuable purpose. For one, we don't carry a scale with us to the grocery. We also don't carry around measurement devices and it's difficult to analyze ingredients at home. Hence we have ingredient lists and other standards to guarantee a baseline of consistency by manufacturers for consumers.

Weights and measures (meant also to cover ingredient lists), nutritional facts, and all other highly functional language on the package provide consistency for consumers to compare their options. This means keeping to minimum type sizes and readability that favors grandma's eyes over little Billy's eyes. To the packaging world, this means regulation and additional time for government oversight. To the consumer world, this is another piece of trust they deposit in their bank account for that brand; break the trust and it gets withdrawn from the account. Do it too often and you'll find yourself with insufficient trust funds in that consumer's world.

Barcodes serve an obvious purpose at the checkout, but they also have an important role in inventory controls, just-in-time distribution, and many other essential phases in the product-to-market process. There, it's been said. Now how do we bend these unruly rules? Just like anything, bending without breaking is achieved through experimentation or knowing precisely where the boundaries

fall. With barcodes, be sure to do a scanner test numerous times if you're using a creative or constrained form of the standard barcode. The amount of time saved at the checkout counter and the fact that many retailers will fine the manufacturer for a barcode mishap should define your boundary. With ingredients, measurements, and weights, there are minimums, required formats, and placement prominence standards. Once you know these you can find ways to be creative with language and other aspects that don't have specific requirements.

Every once in a while, ask your team, "Are we being creative to be creative, or is there a greater purpose for our efforts?" You decide which philosophical path you'd like to take. If you need a reason, here are two: One, the more standard-looking something becomes, the less likely consumers will even notice it. Change it slightly and you create a small discovery for the individual handling the package. And two, never miss an opportunity to bring the brand personality to life.

There are plenty of creative ways to use the barcode as a moment of discovery for the shopper. There are also ways to make a barcode not work at all—a definite no-no.

ORCHESTRATING THE MARKETING MIX

Taking a product to market is one of the ultimate orchestrated events. There are reasons why some insist that the best marketing minds should be familiar with *The Art of War* by Sun Tzu. Taking a product from the thought bubble in the air to the final, successful product is akin to planning a war, hopefully without the death and destruction of real combat. The package is one element in a mix of communications materials with a variety of secondary objectives and a single primary objective: To get this product into the hands of people who will purchase it again and again. From an ad campaign (television, radio, or print) that hits on the key messages, emotional rewards, and key benefits, to a public relations

push to create buzz and have every noteworthy person talking about this new thingamajig, to a promotional plan with coupons, trial offers, and a variety of consumer and retailer incentives to push the product through the channel, to finally, an interactive presence so the brand can mingle with the virtual social world of our global online community—these elements all contribute to the success of the product.

Each of these elements requires a vast amount of specific knowledge and a director who can deftly pull it all together. Gone are the days when the "integrated" agency could serve as director or integrator. Today the management team on the client side needs to manage the brand and therefore has to serve as both director and integrator.

Once an orchestrated approach is understood, then beware of medium bias by the professionals you use or have as advisors. The best way to do this is to inquire into their backgrounds: If they come from advertising, they likely have a bias towards paid advertising in certain forms. If they come from public relations, from direct marketing, or from promotions, they will likely have the corresponding bias toward each of those professions. Now, ask yourself, if someone has a background in guerilla marketing, what then is the bias? It's probably that they prefer getting it done on a grass-roots level with a grab bag of creative tactics combining many of the available mediums. Not a bad bias, and this doesn't mean you avoid all ad people. It just means you should try to avoid having your promotions professionals doing advertising or your ad people doing packaging work. And if you need a good conductor to orchestrate it all, lean toward someone with an eclectic media background.

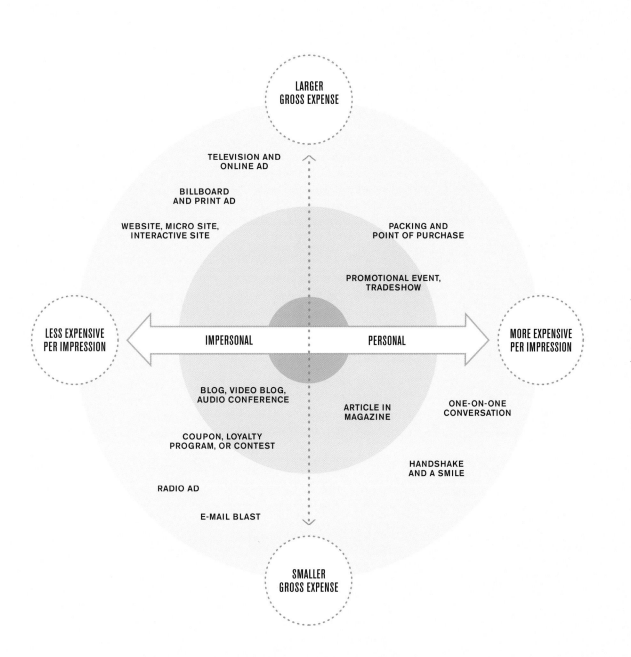

LARGER
GROSS EXPENSE

TELEVISION AND
ONLINE AD

BILLBOARD
AND PRINT AD

WEBSITE, MICRO SITE,
INTERACTIVE SITE

PACKING AND
POINT OF PURCHASE

PROMOTIONAL EVENT,
TRADESHOW

LESS EXPENSIVE
PER IMPRESSION

IMPERSONAL   PERSONAL

MORE EXPENSIVE
PER IMPRESSION

BLOG, VIDEO BLOG,
AUDIO CONFERENCE

ARTICLE IN
MAGAZINE

ONE-ON-ONE
CONVERSATION

COUPON, LOYALTY
PROGRAM, OR CONTEST

HANDSHAKE
AND A SMILE

RADIO AD

E-MAIL BLAST

SMALLER
GROSS EXPENSE

The tools you choose to use should vary by both gross expense of use, cost per impression, and effectiveness of the medium. Fully understand which mediums balance effectiveness (based on how you define it) and efficiency. And if you're not sure, experiment and keep score so you can repeat what works. All things being relative, this chart provides some perspective on the relationship between mediums and expense.

SOURCE: CAPSULE

Packaging Guidelines

THE FENCE ALONGSIDE THE ROAD TO SUCCESS

Spend days, nights, and weekends to create a unique-to-the-world package. It leaves your office, heads for the printer, packager, and then onto the shelf. Now what happens? It comes to life in ads, alongside other packages in product reviews, people talk about it, write about it, and the world starts to take notice. Now everyone wants to be attached to success and add it to their portfolio. The package starts to change. The line of products evolves as other designers find ways to "improve" the package even though it has seen amazing success. Change happens, whether good or bad, and it needs to be managed.

Setting up guidelines is much like designing a fence that runs along a dangerous stretch of road. The comparison extends to the type of car you're driving and whether you're insured to the extent you should be. If the process to create the package only cost a nominal amount, guidelines might not be necessary. If you're driving a new Bentley, you might want to build a strong fence to protect your metaphorical asset.

Now that you've decided to do it, what should be covered in a packaging guidelines document? Start with anything not covered in the corporate brand guidelines and everything important to the consistency of the package design. Start with colors, type, and art before moving to the proper use of the logo and all other intellectual property on the package. The depth of this document should correspond to the number of products in the line and the value of the brand as an asset of the organization.

ITEMS TO CONSIDER:

▸ Why following guidelines is important
▸ Brand attributes
▸ Audiences
▸ Packaging structure
▸ Imagery, illustration, and photography
▸ Language, tone, and style of copy
▸ Graphic structure and layout of packages
▸ Tools to use in packaging design process
▸ Contact person for answers to detailed questions

When the Honeywell brand is put in front of retail buyers, they know the product inside can be trusted to deliver on a promise. When consumers purchases a new product packaged under the Honeywell brand, they expect to trust the product. Consistent delivery with Honeywell means an innovative product and also means a package that delivers the same level of innovation and trust. Guidelines like these set the standard for anyone using the Honeywell brand.

CAPSULE

AIRCRAFT CARRIER IN TEN-FOOT (2.7M) WAVES. PILOT APPROACHES AT 800 FEET (244M). TAIL HOOK DOWN AND ARRESTER GEAR RESET. BREAK TURN AT 4G. WHEELS CONNECT; THE WIRE IS CAUGHT. 250 MPH TO DEAD STOP; SIX SECONDS. JUST AS COMPLEX WITH LESS PROBABILITY OF DEATH: GETTING A PRODUCT FROM A PRODUCER'S DOCK TO A RETAILER'S HOT SPOT.

From Producer to Shelf

What are your competitive advantages when it comes to getting a product from producer to shelf? The fewest products in the channel at any given point, the fewest human touches required, the least weight shipped, and finding your competitive advantage by how efficiently you manage the channel. Today's cost-accounting methods allow us to scrutinize every angle of the distribution channel and determine what parts are eating up margin. Then the ability to drill down into data affords managers amazing access to real-time data. Data, alas, is only a teaspoon in the recipe; creativity and leadership are two heaping cups each.

Creativity is the business term for intuitive design thinking. The sign of a creative mind in business is being able to float above the issues and see how one change in the channel affects any and all other aspects of your distribution. If eighty percent of the profit is in twenty percent of your customers, why do you still work with the other eighty percent? Because if you continue to apply the formula, how many customers would you have? One? How smart is it to use the eighty/twenty rule without considering other implications?

The value of leadership in channel management manifests in the ability to pull the trigger. If all decisions were black and white, the world wouldn't need leaders. Choices would be immediately apparent to anyone with enough book smarts to earn a bachelor's degree. Thankfully, our world is full of color and various shades of gray, and leadership rests on the ability to make decisions that are anything but black and white.

Detailed Delivery

FROM ALLIGATOR TO ZEBRA

Reaching the shelf is a process in itself. Depending on the category, the infinite number of details required to get a packaged product from point of origin to point of sale is astounding. The point A to point B metaphor just doesn't work unless you understand that points C to Z will require equal attention when distributing a packaged product.

If you're wondering how bad it could be, consider this: The way a fold on a box matches with the direction of the paper fiber determines whether the fold score looks cracked and unprofessional. These are the details that won't cause a product to fail on the shelf, but they will undoubtedly make it suffer in the hands of the retailer.

It may feel overwhelming, but when you break down everything, the process starts to feel manageable. Now consider the information flow running concurrently with the physical item in the distribution channel. It quickly turns overwhelming again until the idea of RFID (radio frequency identification) becomes a reality. It's the technological headache reducer you might consider as inventive and lifesaving as aspirin.

STEPS OF THE EXECUTION PROCESS

Now you've done it. The brand strategy is defined. The name is identified and trademarked. The package concepts have been viewed and approved, and refinements have been made. The final package has been tested with consumers and they're ready to buy. The question out of their mouths is loud: "Where and when can I get it?" You are nowhere near the finish, but you are in the race. The appropriate phrase now is, "Bring it home."

Thinking of taking a new product to market? Feeling a bit intimidated? The good news arrives when you discover how many companies, firms, and individuals specialize in logistics/distribution.

The more you know as a designer about each step in the process, the better chance you'll have to influence the execution and delivery of your package. Leave it all up to someone else and you may be disappointed when your package shows up on the shelf. From the client's perspective, keeping the designer involved offers an eye for authenticity when the package and product hit each point in the process. Designers are problem solvers and visual thinkers. Their passion for quality will come through if they are intimately involved throughout the process.

STEP 1

Files to Printer / Proofs

▸ Digital files delivered

▸ Specification documents / Die lines

▸ List prints and color matching on materials

▸ Proofs reviewed by client team

▸ Proofs reviewed by design team

▸ Changes and review again until final

Client: The expense to make changes at this point is much less than when the product hits the shelf and your buyer doesn't like the typo.

Designer: Specifying every detail takes discipline and a fascination with details. You may not think you're responsible until the client comes back asking why you didn't have specific details for the printer. Now you are responsible.

STEP 2

Printing / Press Checks

▸ Material specs matched

▸ Quantities agreed on

▸ Color matching

▸ Photography / Illustration

▸ Match primary to secondary package colors

▸ Ink coverage / Faults in the plates or film

Client: You may not be obligated to attend all press checks, but you need to know who will sign the final approval. With responsibility comes cost, if you absolve yourself of responsibility you had better know to whom you've given it.

Designer: Now is a good time to go back to the original design approved by the client. Does the package reflect what they agreed to produce? Make changes now, don't wait until your client rejects it.

STEP 3

Delivery to Manufacturer / Packing Product

▸ Delivery timing

▸ Storage for inventory

▸ Integrated into manufacturing process

▸ Quality assurance checks / Safety sealing

▸ Just-in-time inventory

Client: Responsibility passes to other suppliers, but it doesn't mean you can't call upon the original designers to solve problems. Most designers are invested in getting a package all the way through the channel; so they have a good story to tell.

Designer: Although these are likely not your areas of expertise, the type of problem shouldn't be restricting. Use your intuitive nature and add valuable perspective to problems that arise.

STEP 4

Consolidating / Shipping

▸ Pallets

▸ Refrigeration / Climate controlled

▸ Truck sizes

▸ Locations

▸ Ship time / Unloading

▸ Pick, pack, and ship to stores

Client: Overlaying the brand meaning can impact the distribution channel. For instance, an environmentally responsible brand doesn't just consider the package; rather every aspect of the channel, product, and messaging.

Designer: Keeping true to the brand now can be challenging. This is where details and timing are essential while other factors fade. Help by keeping your eye on the original objectives.

STEP 5

Merchandising / Selling Through

▸ Unpacking

▸ Shelving

▸ Display adjustments

▸ Price adjustments

▸ Extra inventory

▸ Reporting

Client: Many of these details should fall into place if you've planned for product merchandising. If you don't have a plan, then pick up a magic wand at your local magic shop.

Designer: Checking in when the product is on the shelf can provide nuanced feedback on how well the original plan was executed.

SOURCE: CAPSULE

Review, Assess, Repeat

COMPLETE THE CIRCLE OF LIFE

The modern definition of insanity is endlessly repeating the same behaviors and expecting a different outcome. That said, change for the sake of change is not the answer either. The answer between these two options can be found on the back of most shampoo bottles—three simple steps.

After you've reached a milestone worthy of stopping for an assessment, review what's happened. Take an honest look at each piece of the process and identify the fault lines. If you don't see any and think you've achieved perfection, think again. Look at damaged product or packages. Look at returns and note what happened to your package. Devote some effort to observing how your package is being used, handled, and disposed of when it has reached the end of its useful life.

Assess the hot spots or what might be called "points of pain" coming from retailers or distributors. Not everything can be fixed at once, but fixing some issues may influence other problems. This is where net present value or internal rate of return can be factored in to determine what would result from changes to the package. Incremental change is the standard, but it all depends on how many issues come out of your assessment.

If your channel partners are important to your success, involving them in the process can build a stronger relationship for future product distribution. It can also give the partner more insight into how you do business. And, of course, you will likely be able to learn from their experience to take a leap beyond where the competitive set is lounging around at club complacent.

If your design team needs help seeing the changes, bring them closer to context so they can see how the package is being used and abused.

The visually intuitive design community can see it if it's there to be seen. What you may find is a design team capable of providing process improvement designs to surround a great package with exceptional distribution. At a minimum you'll gain a deeper appreciation for what the package has to endure from the road to the shelf.

Repeat what works and move away from behaviors that do not. Easier said than done, but there are ways to map out a logistics diagram and identify the weak points in the process. Just a simple diagram matched up with a discussion about where your package uses the most amount of energy, where it typically gets lost, or where it comes into contact with dangerous objects will light the way.

Even a priceless package is worthless if it never leaves the shipping box to feel the loving, yet greedy, grasp of a consumer.

PROCESS METHOD

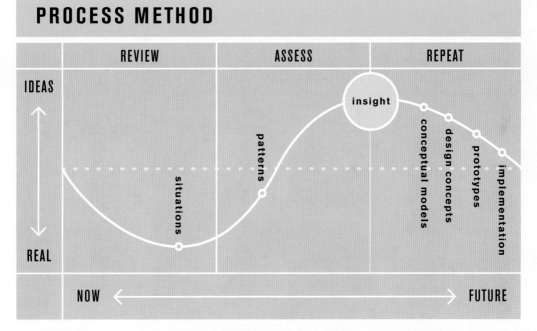

REVIEW	ASSESS	REPEAT

IDEAS

REAL

situations

patterns

insight

conceptual models

design concepts

prototypes

implementation

NOW ← → FUTURE

Seeing the finish line and working with that in mind is one trick. Seeing the next starting line gives an entirely new perspective on how iterative the process needs to be. If you're finished, you're done. If you're building an exceptional brand, you're never done.

SOURCE: CAPSULE

RCES

"THE FUTURE IS HERE. IT'S JUST NOT WIDELY DISTRIBUTED YET."
– WILLIAM GIBSON

PENS FROM 1970, HARD CANDIES IN AND OUT OF THEIR WRAPPERS, AN OVERUSED LINT BRUSH, AND AN OLD CALCULATOR MISSING THE NUMBER TWO. THE FIRST REFERENCE POINT FOR ANYTHING LOST AND ALL THINGS HANDY. IT IS THE MOST RESOURCE-PACKED SPACE IN OUR LIVES, AND IT HUMBLY GOES BY THE NAME "JUNK DRAWER."

The Junk Drawer of Knowledge

When was the last time you dug into your junk drawer? Spend some in time there and you might find some surprising gems. Few of us go to our junk drawer seeking inspiration but we dip in often. When you need to get something done or you've lost something, this is usually the first place you look. Like the reference section of a library, it may not be beautiful or exciting, but it is brimming with helpful information. For our part, we have created this section to provide you with important reference points when you're deep into a packaging project. This is where you find the disciplines, professions, and requirements surrounding smart package design, including language translation, intellectual property, government agencies, and a few other parties interested in the safety and security of the person on the final receiving end of your package design.

Government regulations on the package of products touch on everything from fraudulent products to trademark infringements to the words required on a package entering another country. Languages can have governmental requirements but often the translation of meaning is more important to the success or failure of a package design. It is essential to understand, translate, and adapt to the meaning of language.

Intellectual property laws protect the soft goods like trademarks, copyrights, and patents in the same way that an outer box protects a package during delivery.

Created, expanded, and refined over time, this is the junk drawer that offers important artifacts of knowledge for that occasion when it's most needed.

Languages and Iconography

TEN THOUSAND IMAGES, ONE WORD

Written and visual language, the choreographed dance between the two is an essential talent in design. The written language of a brand, just like that of the visual, needs to convey the personality. Sounds easy, but like any other mixture of languages, translation is required. If the visual language is communicating sophistication and elegance while the written is focused on witty and edgy, a disconnect in the personality may not be obvious, yet. This is where visual studies are a handy tool to translate the visual language into a written one, even before a design is started. Then, consumer testing can pull out any subtleties where language translation was muddy or confusing.

Digging deeper into the relationship we move into hierarchy and how the information is conveyed in a consistent manner on a package and across the entire line of products. Hierarchy offers many elements such as size relationships, visual reference points, and distance between levels of information. Utilizing hierarchy not only helps to clearly communicate essential elements to domestic audiences, it also offers a device for international audiences to more readily translate the package design elements.

The other international language is iconography, or the use of simple illustrations/icons to communicate larger complex ideas, features, or benefits of the product. The use of iconography is common now for international packaging due to the amount of space it saves on a package, but it's still important to test the language to make sure it translates as intended.

Although the most sophisticated hierarchy or iconography can't replace actual "in country" language, it can help tremendously for consumers who wish to find your product on the shelf the second and third time.

International languages on a package can often be met with groans by the design team. Iconography, photography, and color form part of an international language, but the meaning needs interpretation by the appropriate audiences. Move outside the borders of your home country and you'll find many of your global neighbors require domestic language on a package. The great reward of this new marketplace of languages is a need to simplify packaging to a degree capable of handling a minimum of three languages. If you favor the word simplify, there's no better reason to use it in abundance with your clients.

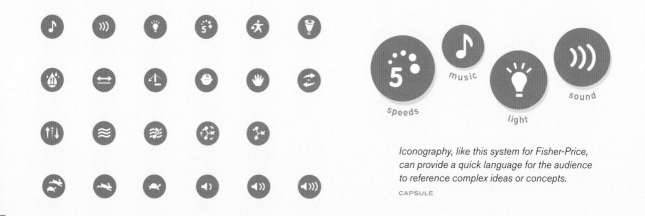

Iconography, like this system for Fisher-Price, can provide a quick language for the audience to reference complex ideas or concepts.

CAPSULE

INTERNATIONAL CONSIDERATIONS

··· **Color** White means clinical in western cultures and death in eastern cultures. The varied meaning should be understood, region by region.

··· **Icons** There are plenty of icons with international meaning. If one doesn't seem to exist, create it yourself and clearly communicate what you intend it to mean. Consider an icon may have contextual meaning, like an Asian icon for rice sold in the Middle East may actually work really well.

··· **Photography** There are many cultural norms such as how you portray women in Middle Eastern countries that need to be considered and respected.

··· **Words** Not all words translate as you intend, using "in country" translators will reduce the risk of insulting someone's mother. Also, consider not every language takes up the same amount of space to say the same thing. German often causes the most surprise when it takes up to 35 percent more space to say the same thing in Spanish.

Governmental Agencies and Legislation

HONESTY IS EVERYONE'S BEST POLICY

Protecting you against yourself. Protecting us against ourselves. Governments are said to exist to protect those who can't protect themselves, and packaging is an area where it is sometimes necessary. Using the United States as an example, there are a few government organizations with whom you'll get quite friendly during the packaging design process. The Food and Drug Administration (FDA) for all food items and over-the-counter drugs; the Bureau of Alcohol, Tobacco and Firearms (ATF) for those items; and the United States Department of Agriculture for poultry, meat, and eggs. The FDA provides guidelines for compliance with labeling, and instructions for use and handling of food and drug related items. The FDA is the agency you'll interact with most, unless you're having real fun conversing with the ATF, for obvious reasons.

These symbols mean please recycle.

These symbols mean 'made from recycled material' and exactly how much.

The information you print on the label must be impossible to remove, so make sure it's legible and comprehensible. The language must match what's spoken in the location, region, or place the product will be sold. There must be a mock-up of the final package submitted to the government agency for approval. And obviously, the package must comply with all regulatory agency requirements in addition to state and federal laws. If you start to wonder where all this knowledge resides, search the World Wide Web and you'll find plenty of sources.

European Union and international laws vary to a great degree within the details, but the ideas remain the same. Government policies are typically set up to protect their citizens from misleading and malicious behaviors by shady manufacturers.

FEDERAL LAWS TO CONSIDER:

▶ To make sure the claims and representations are truthful and honest

▶ To consider the proper protection against damage of the product during handling and shipping

▶ To consider the environmental impact of the package design

▶ To ensure the package is constructed with materials that don't negatively affect the contents

▶ To support the consistent communication of product contents

	PETE ♻1	HDPE ♻2	V ♻3	LDPE ♻4	PP ♻5	PS ♻6	OTHER ♻7
	Polyethylene Terephthalate (PET)	High Density Polyethylene (HDPE)	Polyvinyl Chloride (PVC)	Low Density Polyethylene (LDPE)	Polyproplene (PP)	Polystyrene (PS)	Other Plastics
Properties	1 PETE	2 HDPE	3 V	4 LDPE	5 PP	6 PS	7 Other
Clarity	Clear	Translucent	Clear	Translucent	Translucent	Clear	
Moisture Barrier	Fair to Good	Good to Excellent	Fair	Good	Good to Excellent	Poor to Fair	
Oxygen Barrier	Good	Poor	Good	Poor	Poor	Fair	
Maximum Temperature	120°F 48.8°C	145°F 62.7°C	140°F 60°C	120°F 48.8°C	165°F 73.8°C	150°F 65.5°C	
Rigidity	Moderate to High	Moderate	Moderate to High	Low	Moderate to High	Moderate to High	
Resistance to Impact	Good to Excellent	Good to Excellent	Fair to Good	Excellent	Fair to Good	Fair to Good	
Resistance to Heat	Poor to Fair	Good	Poor to Fair	Fair	Good	Fair	
Resistance to Cold	Good	Excellent	Fair	Excellent	Poor to Fair	Poor	
Resistance to Sunlight	Good	Fair	Poor to Fair	Fair	Fair	Poor to Fair	

Intellectual Property

GET YOUR HANDS OFF MY TRADE DRESS

Success is often copied, sometimes without regard for what parts can be legally duplicated. When it comes to the essential assets surrounding a package design, there are tools to keep copycat competitors from getting too close. Trademarks, patents, copyrights, and trade secrets—these are all legal tools you should understand how to wield if you're creating package designs.

Patents apply to processes, formulas, and machines as well as method and designs. The strengths in a patent come from the fact that you have proven that your patented item is unique while not having to use it in commerce for the patent to be effective. The weaknesses are that you are required to show the item in all its detail to the patent office in order to prove uniqueness, and a patent gives you only twenty years of protection. Although patents are fairly inexpensive to obtain if you have something unique, defending them against infringers is another matter entirely and typically involves a significantly larger dollar amount.

Trademarks apply to name, shape, logo, symbol, color, or any combination of shapes and elements that come together to be trademarked. When considering whether you can own a color, trademark is the legal tool that allows you to claim that ownership. This also applies to the other items of a design. The purpose of a trademark is to avoid confusion between products and brands; hence, you will need to prove to the trademark office that the registration you're submitting is not confusingly similar to anything else on the market. Then you're required to use the trademarked asset in commerce. The strength is that a trademark can last indefinitely, can be obtained very inexpensively, and can keep your competitors from "borrowing" the brand assets you've created. The weakness is the requirement to use it in commerce.

Copyright covers the original written words of a brand personality. It is most often associated with books, but it also applies to package copywriting, advertising, music, and other original works of art. Copyright is by far the least expensive legal device to use, but it can offer substantial protection against importers using your original work on knock-off products.

Trade secrets have to be the most mysterious of all the legal devices, hence the name. They are defined as the formulas, thinking, processes, plans, ingredients, and any company property not in the public domain. Trade secrets are a major reason you are asked to sign nondisclosure or confidentiality agreements with clients. Keeping the formula for Coca-Cola under wraps is the most visible example of a trade secret. Essentially this tool is valuable for keeping things that are meant to be confidential entirely confidential. Trade secrets last as long as you can keep them secret and they have very little cost. That is, until you need to quickly search out someone who has walked out the front door with the family recipe.

Legal advice is worth the price you pay, unless you pay too much. Find an intellectual property (IP) lawyer you can afford and trust; they can offer valuable advice and filing suggestions when considering legal protections. The best and most painful lesson you'll learn is the inability to protect something after it has lost its uniqueness in the marketplace. Seek legal protection early and often —a reasonable investment will be returned to you when you are able to keep competitors out while continuing to be uniquely competitive in the marketplace.

Copyright can discourage competitors from making the same unique claims you do on your package.

"Just copy the ingredients from our competitor's package. It's the same ingredients."

"My child picked the colors for our package. Is that okay?"

"Why do we have to wait for the testing? I just want my package on the shelf."

"Are you in the business of making things look pretty?"

"Why can't we borrow from their packaging design? What will it matter?"

"Can we get a playful feeling without being so darn playful?"

TUDIES

"THE POSITION OF THE ARTIST IS HUMBLE.
HE [OR SHE] IS ESSENTIALLY A CHANNEL."
— PIET MONDRIAN

THE CLIENT: FOX RIVER SOCKS

DESIGN FIRM: CAPSULE (USA)

Right: The sock packaging was designed first and became the centerpiece of the entire campaign to launch a line of Shucking Awesome socks.

Fox River Socks

SHUCKING AWESOME CORN SOCKS

The feeling of putting a good pair of socks on cold feet can be a special moment in someone's day. The Fox River Sock Company has more than a hundred years of experience giving customers those little moments of joy. Their socks have gone to the moon and have reinforced many a foot fetish. Still manufactured in northern Iowa, they offer a great example of sustainable, community-focused manufacturing that confidently defies most MBA analytics. This and many other heroic brand stories were not being sung from the tops of mountains. That needed to change.

PLANNING

The world's first corn sock is completely sustainable and annually renewable. To sock industry geeks, corn fiber technology was revolutionary, earth-shattering stuff. To average consumers, it was still just socks. Albeit, socks with corn in them. The goal was to launch a product that would grab shoppers' attention and intrigue them long enough to get educated on the technology's unique benefits. Capsule sent Fox River some homework to kick off the process. Two weeks later, Fox River sent back the mother load. Scattered throughout the brand history sections, tucked between fiftieth anniversaries and factory expansions, were mentions of sock monkeys, arctic treks, Olympic games, and space odysseys. Fox River was sitting on a gold mine. Its history was extraordinary but had gone unsung for more than a century.

Shucking Awesome socks made from a renewable source of energy. The farm fields and rural culture of where Fox River socks is located were a large influence on the package design concepts.

CREATING

Capsule made it clear that Fox River should push the envelope. Fox agreed. Armed with the findings from planning sessions, Capsule created packaging and communications tying the corn sock story into Fox River's history. Thus, corn socks became more than just a product. Corn socks became a verification of Fox River's vast, quirky tradition—part of its Midwest personality. A distinct and interesting facet of a remarkable brand story that people could relate to and want to make part of their world.

IMPLEMENTING

Fox River's corn sock packaging made a big splash at the 2006 Outdoor Retailer show. The new product line not only hauled in loads of international orders, it resurrected interest in the overall Fox River brand. By tying Fox River's history into the corn socks, audiences who thought they knew everything there was to know gave Fox River a second look.

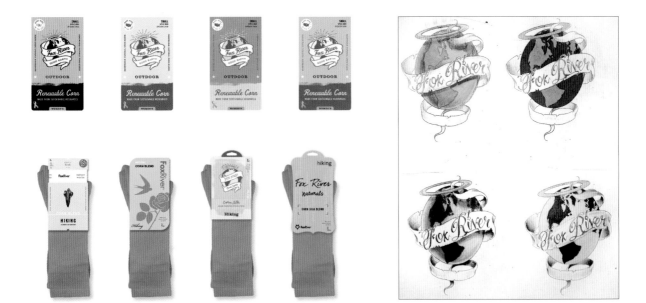

The "Made with Corn" insignia became a product feature identifier at retail and was used as a fun give-away in tattoo form at tradeshows and events.

The package and brand launched at a large outdoor retail event in Salt Lake City, Utah, USA. One pair of socks was shipped to each potential buyer and if they came to the event wearing the socks, they were rewarded.

THE CLIENT: METHOD HOME

DESIGN FIRM: METHOD HOME (USA)

Method Home

OPTION OF METHOD OR MADNESS, PICK METHOD

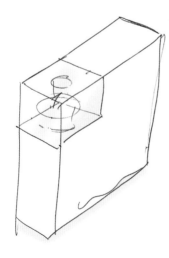

Method home is quickly becoming a household name with household items. As a business, method has founding principles with a dedication to contemporary design thinking. The rocket ship item, designed by the infamous Karim Rashid, sent method products into every designer household in every available market. It has since garnered greater appeal with the mass market, the laggards. This new crowd has picked up on how the design of something can beautify their home in use and while resting on a countertop. Now method has numerous product lines from floor cleaning and laundry detergent to hair care and body wash products.

PLANNING

The offices of method can thank this project for contributing "Don't pull a Bloq on me" to the culture and conversation. It started with a promise that method founder Eric Ryan made to their largest client, Target. In the heat of July, he said, "Sure, we can get a body wash product on the shelves by the holiday season." That was coupled with a desire to create a package that defies conformation by not standing up as most bottle designs would. This became one of those stories where planning does not seem to exist, but in reality, the experience of the team serves the role of research and strategy. There isn't enough time for thoughtful, deliberate, insightful planning; guts, brains, and experience will need to suffice.

Iterative design can wander deliberately or otherwise in many directions. From pebble concepts to a Bloq, providing us with a great example of the leaps iterative design is allowed to take.

The Bloq package stands up to any other body wash package on the market. It is a great example of a unique closure and a package with elegant ergonomics.

CREATING

The charge by Ryan is, "I want a package that won't stand up like every standard package in every bathroom." Where do you go from there? Pebbles, of course. Pebbles, or rather small rocks, don't stand up, but if you pile a few together, they make a nice organic display of product. As the design team developed this idea, it gained quick acceptance and even early praise as an elegant design solution to the challenge. However, as any design process should be iterative, this one ran into the iterative monkey known as "cost to produce." The necessary price point would likely slip right past a Target shopper. Although this wasn't apparent until the Bloq happened, someone needed to stand up for the price point. The result was what is now called "Pulling a Bloq," as the design director, Josh Handy, is now credited with doing.

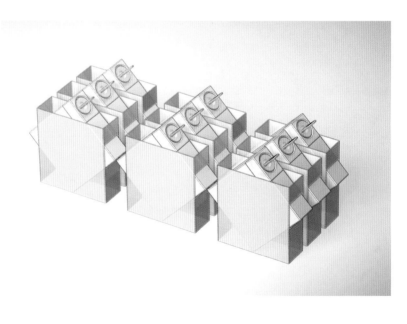

Method is not the first to do this, but it's one of the most recent to win accolades for taking hand soap and putting it on display for all houseguests to see. Much of what method has designed are products that were once hidden in a closet or beneath a sink, now on display for all to appreciate.

IMPLEMENTING

With the price point within sight, the implementation deadline could now be achieved. The team still had to produce the design, get it manufactured, filled, shipped, and on the shelves in what most designers would consider an unrealistic deadline. The rubber met the road and product was delivered on time, and the cool breeze at the end of this sprint relay race was product launch success both financially and emotionally. The method culture now contained another story of how their approach to product development works. Target had another selling product. And the world had another story of design improving everyday lives.

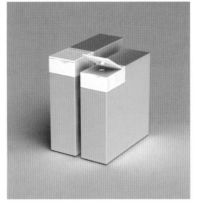

Digital renderings can convey how a closure will work as well as how each package will relate to its pair while on display. They can also be a low-cost option in comparison to physical prototypes when working on the early package concepts.

THE CLIENT: PLUM ORGANICS

DESIGN FIRM: BRAND ENGINE (USA)

Plum Organics

SQUARE AND PLUM EQUALS YUMMY

PLANNING

"Analysis paralysis." We've all heard of it and some even live it on a daily basis. Planning can be a freeway you get on and off quickly to reach your destination faster, as well as looking smarter when you arrive. Planning can also be that country dirt road that doesn't have a turnoff for nearly 100 kilometers. The talent is seeing the road ahead before you enter and knowing when to use your blinker. A robust planning process teamed with a flexible facilitator can be two positive indicators that you're on the right road. The planning team for Brand Engine makes a great match with Plum Organics. Both have a significant amount of knowledge and neither was afraid to learn something new about the baby food category. With this setup, planning for the Plum Organics line had a great chance to deliver a brand to its destination (shelves) and to look good when it got there (obvious).

The face no one could resist, packaging organic cereal that many have had trouble resisting. This package makes a promise: organic, healthy, yummy, and smart baby food. The product lives up to the promise of the package.

Stacking up a flavor selection allows you to see how the hierarchy works, using the spoon as a subtle yet essential communication device. The idea is that a photo can say much more than words, and in this case these words are whispered at a shelf where everyone else is screaming.

CREATING

The designers explored a number of concepts with the client. They refined a couple and arrived at something close to what you see. The result was a package able to convey three powerful points—the innocence of childhood, the comfort of something organic, and the feeling of food even adults would eat. All this is fine and good when you look at the package and say, "Yes it does look good, beautiful, and safe." But the creative process becomes a gold mine when the results, or rather shoppers, start showing up at the shelves.

Alternative concepts give an idea of where the package design could have gone. Each permutation provides its own feel for how the brand would come to life.

IMPLEMENTING

Baby food could be seen as a tired category with a small field of typical competitors putting out line extensions until the cows come home. The Plum Organics line approached the category, packaging, and product development from a beautiful angle. The result was a package and product parents would be happy to pull off the shelf. It delivered other unexpected results when Brand Engine discovered a significant number of adults consuming certain flavors and not hiding the fact from the researchers.

THE CLIENT: INEKE

DESIGN FIRM: HELENA SEO DESIGN (USA)

Right: Authentically blending materials like glass, metal, and plastic creates a feeling of substance with just the right sense of thoughtful style.

Ineke Perfume

THE SCENT OF STYLE AND ELEGANCE

PLANNING

Setting a flag in the sands of time to represent a new view of perfume. Companies who specialize in the science behind olfactory sensory experiences design most perfumes. Fashion models and celebrities are often the only brand names on these perfumes. The connection between the designer of the perfume and the consumer is lost. The new Ineke perfume was designed without a model, fashion brand, or other diva in mind. It was designed with the consumer in mind. The package design needed to reflect this while still capturing the elegance and exclusivity most often attached to the diva with the big name.

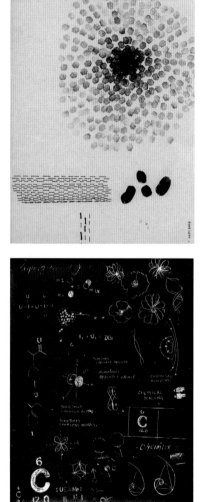

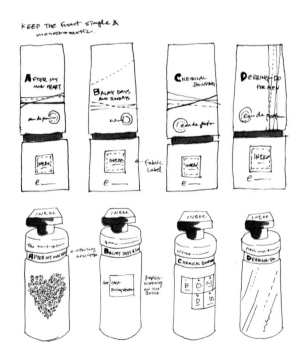

CREATING

Starting with both the visual and written language of the brand, Helena Seo walked the Ineke team through a process of listing words and collecting images. These were used to build the feeling around the perfume's story. Then individual packages were designed to help further visualize the story. After the exterior carton was done, the bottle followed suit within the design language created. There were challenges when it came to finding stock photography that would convey the right message and then having to jump to original photography to get the right feel. The design eventually came together like a three-dimensional puzzle.

Early sketches and art can provide both inspiration and start to provide focus for where the eventual design will go.

Pencil sketches in our digital age continue to be valuable when considering the feeling of an early design. With the right people viewing these sketches you can get more clear direction from your client.

IMPLEMENTING

With an exhaustive knowledge of packaging materials (glass etching, metal engraving, woven labels, etc), Ineke was able to collaboratively pull together and deliver a stunning package for perfume. The lack of a model, diva, or superstar goes unnoticed after the consumer is able to connect with the scent and make it part of her life.

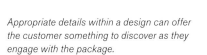

Appropriate details within a design can offer the customer something to discover as they engage with the package.

THE CLIENT: LUXELAB

DESIGN FIRM: DUSTIN ARNOLD (USA)

LuxeLab Blonde-Aid

SMARTER THAN THE AVERAGE BLONDE

Do blondes really have more fun? If so, do they need more help being blonde? This brand identified an unmet need that any brunette would turn up a nose to: helping blondes care for their specific hair color. If there was a need to give blondes a greater advantage, this product was formulated to service that need. The package design had to gracefully convey the help the product was offering this underserved segment.

PLANNING

Planning for such a product required significant scientific discovery and experimentation before a package could even be considered. Then, after dedicating so much time to the product, the package couldn't go unnoticed. It would be like cutting off your nose to spite your face: great product, hideous package. The planning included research from LuxeLab's team as well as anything the designer could find in secondary markets. Once the product formulation was complete and a brand strategy was clear, the creative process could begin.

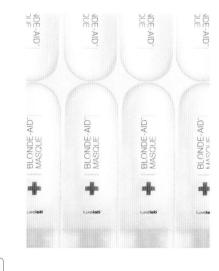

How a package interacts and creates a pattern in collaboration with more of the same packages can go beyond a photograph on the page. It can be a valuable tool to create a billboard effect at the point of display. The LuxeLab package achieves this in an elegant manner.

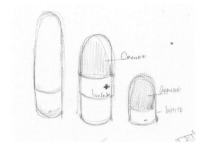

CREATING

Creating something to safely treat hair has many metaphors that work to tell the story. The designer chose to focus on medicinal metaphors surrounding the Red Cross; medical cleanliness; and elegant, simple shapes. The result, after many concepts and many more refinements, was a package design that feels healthy, blonde, and medical.

IMPLEMENTING

Getting a product to the shelf can involve a series of potholes on the long road to market. Although there are plenty of reasons for why blondes don't really need additional caring for their hair, this product has a interesting angle with its focus on blondes. And launching LuxeLab in Southern California, a market bubbling over with candidates, is a whip smart strategy. And in case you're wondering, the product works for converted blondes, too—we asked.

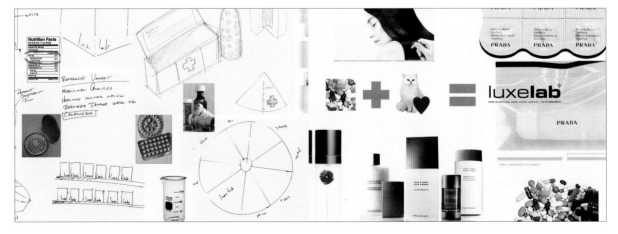

Seeing both sketches and inspirational images gives a glimpse into the minds of everyone involved in this effort. Capturing the history of anything allows us to better understand the depth of work required to bring it to life.

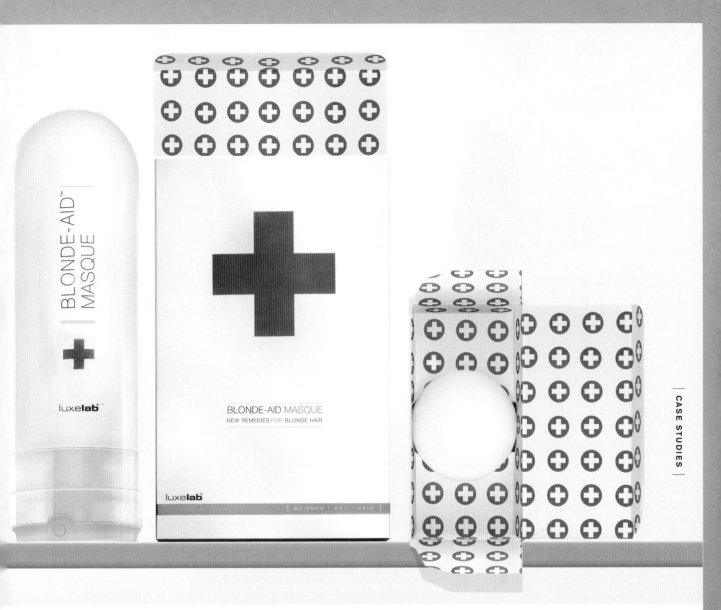

BLONDE-AID™ MASQUE

BLONDE-AID™ MASQUE
NEW REMEDIES FOR BLONDE HAIR

luxe**lab**

SCIENCE · ART · HAIR

By the time a potential shopper views this package, excessive messages and clutter will have little or no effect. The clean design of the secondary packages contribute to the design and a shopper's experience with this package. For that matter, what retailer would hide this beautiful package on the bottom shelf?

THE CLIENT: OLD NASSUA IMPORTS

DESIGN FIRM: CAPSULE (USA)

Right: From the experience of uncapping the bottle, to pouring a shot, to actual consuming the alcohol was a designed experience. The bottle created a unique experience exclusively designed for those who could afford this super-premium vodka brand.

Double Cross Vodka

DISTILLED PERFECTION IN A SQUARE BOTTLE

From distant lands we bring liquids to markets where everyone can enjoy the fruits and grains of labor. Vodka is made from many ingredients, but the distillation and filtration process is really what distinguishes one product from another. That is, until a brand name, identity, and package are created to announce from the tallest point in Slovakia, "We are not like all the others." Old Nassau Imports sought to create a vodka product and brand with enough confidence to boast from any mountain top.

PLANNING

Taking a swim in the marketplace for vodka may seem like an adventure worth taking, but it becomes real work when you've seen your hundredth spirit bottle. The planning process for the team at Old Nassau Imports and Capsule included enough secondary and qualitative research to make an MBA proud. The use of visual language boards helped coalesce the brand language and inspire the rest of the creative process. The result was exactly what planning should accomplish: a better understanding of the risks and rewards, along with a pathway to navigate around the risks.

Visual style boards can be valuable discussion items to translate both vision to reality and visual language to written words. These boards helped the Capsule team create a bottle design to evoke the luxury brand their client desired.

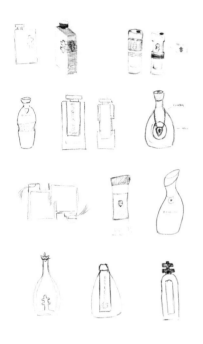

CREATING

Starting with pencil sketches, images of perfume bottles, and mountaintop photos of Slovakia, the creative process had all the right inspiration. The concepts were taken to three-dimensional renderings at an early stage so Old Nassau Imports could take home a short movie and look at the presence of each bottle concept. Early decisions on bottle shape and structure led to innovative cap ideas and a variety of other fundamental bottle design elements. Then graphics were applied to the bottle, taking what was a twenty-fifth-century bottle design back a hundred years to incorporate the heritage of Slovakian culture. The result is a bottle that not only blends old and new but also creates the starkest contrast between those two worlds. This contrast conveys the idea of Double Cross in graphic and dimensional form. The bottle becomes the brand and the brand becomes the bottle.

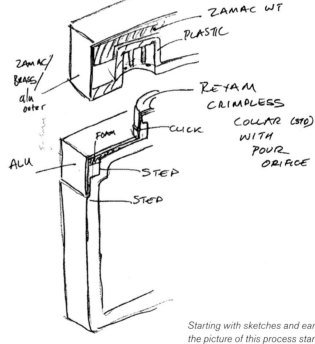

Starting with sketches and early renderings, the picture of this process starts to fill in. From a concept with a removable wristband to an explicit double cross by the bottle design, these early concepts had significant influence on where the bottle ended up.

IMPLEMENTING

Try telling your dream to someone the next morning and sometimes you're met with a curious frown. Putting the concept in front of manufacturers charged with producing the bottle, you could feel the frowns through the conference call. When challenged, the bottle suppliers who could see beyond the constraints and make this dream a reality were the same ones who landed the implementation contract. The process of refinements, implementation, and getting the bottle to the shelf requires truckloads of patience and persistence. Fortunately for everyone, the entire team had plenty of both.

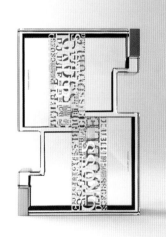

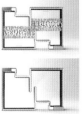

Calligraphy is an old art form which offers an elegant contrast for a modern, clean bottle design. The use of a Slovakian poem on the bottle in this lettering creates an "oh, of course" feeling for the patron loyal to this vodka brand.

The amazing possibilities of digital renderings, which are eventually turned into short movies, can make the process of deciding on your next bottle design as rewarding as watching an academy award winner in Hollywood. These highly rendered concepts allowed the decision makers to immerse themselves in their choices.

THE CLIENT: OUTSET

DESIGN FIRM: OUTSET DESIGN (USA)

Right: A thing of beauty is effortlessly, photogenic. This package design, like a supermodel, is easy on the eyes—both in a photograph and when it goes on display at your local retailer.

Outset Chillware
COOL ENOUGH TO CHILL IN

PLANNING

Love method? Looking for the same passion for design with your grilling utensils and accessories? Hello, Outset. Planning for design in Outset has many of the same organic methods and practices. When it comes to a new product, as the idea develops, it becomes clear where the product will fit in the portfolio, market, and within consumer grilling experiences. It doesn't mean there are months spent on focus groups, surveys, or other massive quantitative research projects. It does mean, however, that strategy is mapped out based on the team's current knowledge, assumptions are made, and the brand vision comes to life in how the product and package are designed.

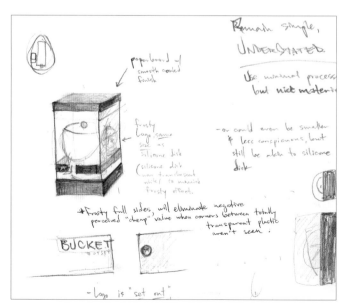

Pencil sketches can quickly lead to solid ideas. The team for Outset was also able to look back on where the package originated with these early sketches.

Everything a master griller would need—yes, everything. The package is efficient and works within the larger design language of the brand.

CREATING

The design process for the Outset team included concept work and rigorous education around what would make a great package design. The packaging design process can sometimes be crushed by a timeline closer to what it takes to cook a hot dog than what it should take to design a package. When faced with this kind of deadline, the Outset design team was able to adapt and still produce a design balancing form and function.

Deep understanding of the context of sale and use can be an essential thread to any design. The Outset packaging was designed with the context of product display in mind. The box has a bellyband that is easily removed to allow storeowners to withdraw one sample without damaging the original package. The product also merchandises like a supermodel with translucent areas allowing the shopper to see nearly all the details inside the package.

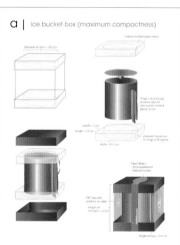

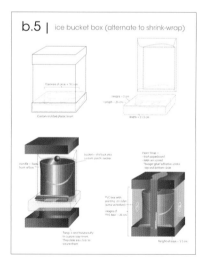

Engineering something beautiful should be as elegant as the design when you understand how it all came together. Engineering the ice bucket isn't the Brooklyn Bridge, but it still has to carry its own weight.

IMPLEMENTING

Getting the product to shelf can have many more details than many management teams are patient enough to handle. Getting it to the shelf and displayed in a "you know you want me" sort of way requires more than just patience, it requires a bit of art. The Outset ice bucket with its display ready design was a great addition to an already thorough list of grilling and entertaining items. The new package fit into the line and stood out like all the other products in the Outset portfolio. Give a retailer something they can sell and they'll be happy. Give them something that sells itself and they may just sing a joyful song. Outset continues to bring great products to happy retailers.

Nothing exists in a vacuum—especially not a product surrounded by just as many complementary items in the brand portfolio. Making sure it all works together is the brand owner's responsibility and the task of creating consistency will likely sit firmly atop the designer's shoulders.

THE CLIENT: REVOLUTION TEA

DESIGN FIRM: REVOLUTION TEA (USA)

Revolution Tea

ANYTHING BUT AN EVOLUTION IN TEA

How do you start a revolution without firing a shot? Start with a tea bag and loose tea leaves and infuse your passion for tea. That's the formula used by Revolution Tea and judging from their success, it seems we should adopt their interpretation of a revolution. When all you have is your package, your package has to become all that you are. Revolution has achieved this with elegance and style.

PLANNING

Highly accurate and descriptive intuition is essential to any planning effort. Revolution Tea relied on existing knowledge and a belief that they needed to create exclusivity around their teas. This effort led to a strategy focused on creating passionate brand advocates for their tea. The plan was inspired by other great brands like Tazo, Apple, and Clinique that have proven their ability to elevate their brand with advocates and exceptional design.

Noticing the details isn't just a designer's role today. If you spend time with a package, you, the consumer, notice the color coding, the simple hierarchy of type and images, and the tin cap that's color coded with the "R" to signal your tea when the package gets merchandised on its side. Design details are not just for designers anymore; they can have significant influence when thoughtfully considered.

CREATING

Using process as the foundation, the Revolution Tea design team used a fluid and flexible framework to create engaging packaging design concepts. The workflow process was designed to eliminate chaos, even with tight deadlines. This comes from a belief system that focuses more on professional communicators, marketers, and planners rather than the hero artist who generates magic for all to admire. The result gets admired by heroes and teams alike for what it does on the shelf and in consumers' homes.

Not everyone in the world believes in Revolution Tea, so you might not find it everywhere. Personalize your tea experience and bring your own small tin. Then your favorite restaurant can charge you for a mug of hot water, and you can design your own revolution.

IMPLEMENTING

Working with a variety of shapes, forms, materials, and printing technologies requires significant knowledge and patience when implementation time comes. The Revolution Tea brand has been implemented across so many mediums and materials. Their team philosophy shows us all how much can be done by an authentic team versus one person's vast knowledge of many subject areas. Go team.

Can you taste the product before you even touch the package? This might be a high hurdle to clear, but when you look at the Revolution packages, they make the mouth-watering part seem easy.

THE CLIENT: MICROSOFT, WINDOWS VISTA

DESIGN FIRM: STRUCTURAL: SMART DESIGN (USA)
               PACKAGING: HORNALL ANDERSON DESIGN WORKS (USA)

Microsoft Windows Vista

STRUCTURED TO REVEAL AN EXPERIENCE

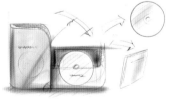

When was the last time you heard someone say, "We need some out-of-the-box thinking here"? Did you find yourself screaming on the inside? Or did you laugh to yourself and make it sound like a cough? But when you're talking about the box and the largest software company in the known universe, a bit of gray matter outside the box is precisely what was needed.

PLANNING

This effort was launched with exhaustive research on materials, consumer behaviors, and some proprietary research methods that you'd have to commit a crime to extract from Smart Design. Transforming the Microsoft Windows software box needed to start with a better understanding of where the world was going, as this software was facing a global marketplace. And it needed to be as revolutionary as the software it contained. The bar was set high, but it was balanced by the fact that Microsoft software wasn't known for revolutionary packaging. Smart Design's opportunity was clear.

Although there is nothing like a real prototype when making a packaging decision, sketches can be a great way to get focus and agreement on a direction. Generally speaking, the more complex an idea, the more details in the early sketches—exemplified by these Smart Design sketches.

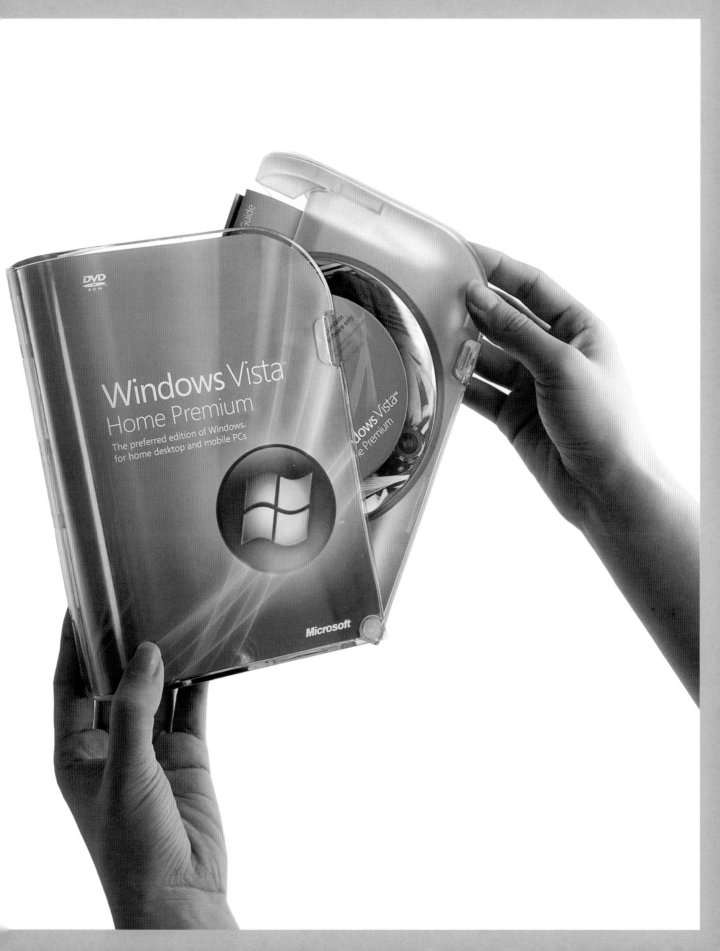

CREATING

Designing unique graphics on a rectangular box wouldn't be reason enough to hire the firm best known for designing the OXO product line. The Smart Design team was set to re-create the software package experience by designing a unique package structure.

The reveal of something new is core to the packaging experience and this new reveal couldn't help but get a Window's fanatic excited about Vista, the new operating system. The translucent plastics reflected the translucent design of the software itself.

IMPLEMENTING

There are many ways to measure success in life and the same goes for packaging design. If you see a design used once and then never applied again, you're likely looking at a disappointment. In the case of the Smart Design structure for Microsoft Windows Vista, the result was just the opposite. This new structure became the standard for many other packaged software coming from this global brand. Showing us the real story here, the packaging experience should be designed to reveal and exemplify the contents packaged.

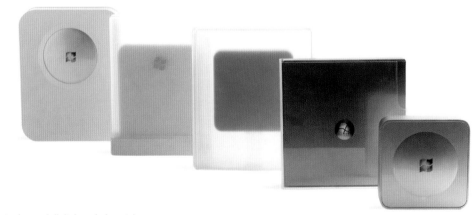

Rapid prototyping and digital renderings take a package to another level and allow greater interaction with the concept. The result is better understanding and hopefully better decisions.

THE CLIENT: COCA-COLA COMPANY

DESIGN FIRM: TURNER DUCKWORTH (UK)

The Coca-Cola Company, Tab Energy

REVITALIZED TO RE-ENERGIZE ANOTHER GENERATION

Many high-value, hardworking brands have been retired as organizations attempt to cut costs and consolidate and reduce expenses. There will come a day when revitalizing those retired brands becomes fashionable. Organizations will venture into their brand attic to find gems they can dust off, shine up, and reintroduce to a new generation. Oh wait, that day is here; thank you, Coca-Cola.

PLANNING

Although it wasn't completely retired, the Tab brand had moved to Florida, bought some property, and started eating dinner at four in the afternoon. When Turner Duckworth was given the task of a reintroduction, most of the Tab brand meaning was focused around the associations of a '70s and '80s low-calorie soft drink marketplace in the United States. This wasn't a hindrance as the brand would now be known as a fruity energy drink for modern, stylish women.

The historical typography used for the Tab logo is brought forward through the current design. Although change is good, carrying the heritage of this brand forward delivers credibility and trust.

Tab Energy showcase
Energy drinks sell to one objective: instant win imagery.

Tab Energy point of clarity
No wonder that for many women, energy is about building and toning their legs, for them, Tab takes a simple twist to be an end of a sense experience as a sub sub of shoes. It's a fashion accessory.

Tab Energy design idea
Tab concept design was inspired by the fashion structure and a sub set of women and the second sense created for fashion industry. The result was pattern boosting.

CREATING

The design of the new primary and secondary packaging was given a fashionable trade dress borrowing directly from the popular optical illusion of dots that seem to disappear as the package moves. This design strategy takes an emphasis away from the logo and creates a feeling of modern energy. For those who would have seen the old Tab, this new design would certainly spark curiosity. With the next generation, the package fits right into the subcultures for young women with a sense of style.

IMPLEMENTING

Starting with a smaller, energy-drink-sized can and going all the way to a secondary package and a detailed identity system for the brand, the package had precise implementation. The results start to show up when the little pink can hits the streets and ends up in celebrity hands. Then the clubs start adding it to vodka drinks like the Stiletto Confession made from orange liqueur, vodka, pineapple juice—and the new pink packaged Tab. It may not bump Red Bull from its entrenched position in the clubs, but it has carved out a cozy niche and made a promising start.

Tab Energy design exploration
Designers in San Francisco and London created a range of options that were ruthlessly edited, presented to the client, refined and researched.

Pink has tremendous meaning and trades on the history of and nostalgia for the Tab brand. Combining heritage and modern imagery offers a glimpse into how the design team used passion and ingenuity to resurrect this great brand.

GALLER

Y

"DESIGN IS THE TRIBUTE ART PAYS
TO INDUSTRY." — PAUL FINCH

1.

2.

3.

4.

1. CLIENT: B.T. MCELTRATH FIRM: CAPSULE (USA) DESIGNER: GREG BROSE 2. CLIENT: PROCTER & GAMBLE FIRM: NICE LTD (USA) DESIGNER: BOKSIL
KIM CHOI 3. CLIENT: PEPSI FIRM: T.B.D./HATCH DESIGN (USA) DESIGNER: KATIE JAIN 4. CLIENT: SCANBECH FIRM: ULFELDT SELLE16 (DENMARK)
DESIGNERS: JENS ULFELDT

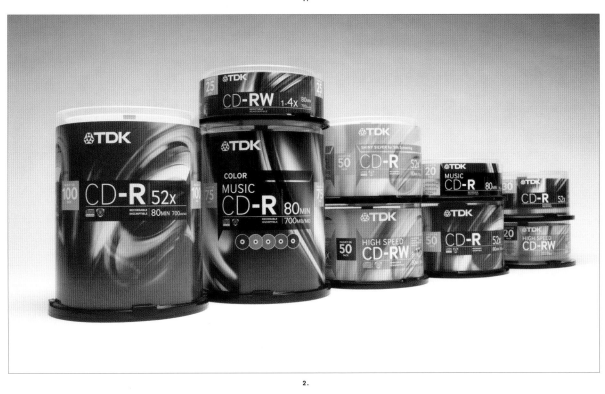

1.

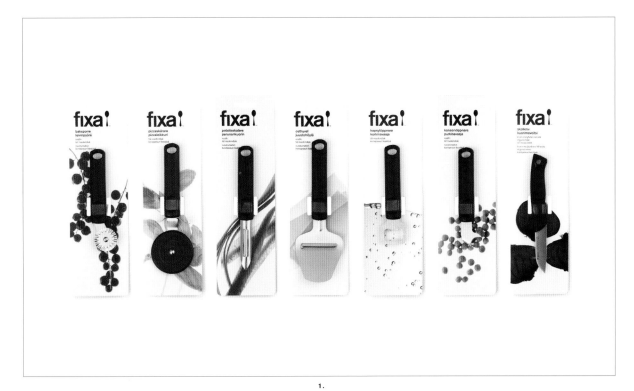

2.

1. CLIENT: AXFOOD/FIXA FIRM: BVD (SWEDEN) DESIGNER: KINA GIESENFELD HERNER **2.** CLIENT: TDK ELECTRONICS CORPORATION
FIRM: INTERROBANG DESIGN COLLABORATIVE (USA) DESIGNER: MARK SYLVESTER

CLIENT: SHU UEMURA FIRM: BERGMAN ASSOCIATES (USA) DESIGNER: ROBERT BERGMAN

CLIENT: COCA-COLA BLÃK FIRM: PEARLFISHER (UNITED KINGDOM) DESIGNER: SHAUN BOWEN

1.

2.

3.

4.

1. CLIENT: DELICIOUS BRANDS FIRM: CAHAN & ASSOCIATES (USA) DESIGNER: ERIK ADAMS **2.** CLIENT: HERMAN MILLER FIRM: FUSEPROJECT (USA) DESIGNERS: YVES BEHAR AND TIM KENNEDY **3.** CLIENT: COSTA FOODS FIRM: CARTER WONG TOMLIN (UK) DESIGNERS: PHIL CARTER AND CHLOE VICARY **4.** CLIENT: YOUNG & RUBICON FIRM: HARCUS DESIGN (AUSTRALIA) DESIGNER: MELONIE RYAN

1.

2.

1. CLIENT: ROCAMOJO FIRM: EVENSON DESIGN GROUP (USA) DESIGNER: KERA SCOTT **2.** CLIENT: MCKENZIE RIVER CORPORATION FIRM: TURNER DUCKWORTH (UK) DESIGNER: ANTHONY BILES

CLIENT: OFFICEMAX FIRM: GRAVITY TANK, INC (USA) DESIGNERS: SCOTT TERNOVITS AND MORITSUGU KARIYA

1.

2.

1. CLIENT: THE SUGAR PLUM FAIRY BAKING COMPANY FIRM: CRAVE, INC. (USA) DESIGNERS: LAURA ANDREWS AND RUSS MARTIN **2.** CLIENT: BOA HOUSEWARES FIRM: TURNER DUCKWORTH (UK) DESIGNER: ANTHONY BILES

1.

2.

1. CLIENT: MADE IN WASHINGTON STORES FIRM: KENDALL ROSS (USA) DESIGNER: CHARLIE WORCESTER 2. CLIENT: THE NORTH FACE FIRM: SATELITE DESIGN (USA) DESIGNER: AMY GUSTINCIC

1.

2.

3.

4.

1. CLIENT: HOOD RIVER DISTILLERS FIRM: LEOPOLD KETEL & PARTNERS (USA) 2. CLIENT: TRUE FRUITS FIRM: TRUE FRUITS GMBH (GERMANY)
DESIGNERS: JUGA KOSTER AND NICHOLAS LECLOUX 3. CLIENT: SHANGO RUM LIQUEUR FIRM: WALLACE CHURCH, INC. (USA) DESIGNER: MARCO
ESCALANTE 4. CLIENT: PADDYWAX FIRM: PRINCIPLE (USA) DESIGNERS: PAMELA ZUCCKER AND JENNIFER SUKIS

1.

2.

3.

4.

1. CLIENT: OVER THE HILL ORCHARD FIRM: BRADBURY BRANDING & DESIGN (CANADA) DESIGNER: CATHARINE BRADBURY 2. CLIENT: SQUARE ONE ORGANIC VODKA FIRM: MICHAEL OSBORNE DESIGN (USA) DESIGNERS: MICHAEL OSBORNE AND ALICE KOSWARA 3. CLIENT: FOSTER'S AUSTRALIA FIRM: HOYNE DESIGN (AUSTRALIA) DESIGNER: FELICITY DAVISON 4. CLIENT: SANS & SANS FIRM: SONSOLES LLORENS DISSENY GRAFIC (SPAIN) DESIGNER: SONSOLES LLORENS

CLIENT: MADDY'S ORGANIC MEALS FIRM: FUNNEL: ERIC KASS: UTILITARIAN + COMMERCIAL + FINE: ART (USA) DESIGNER: ERIC KASS

1.

2.

3.

4.

1. CLIENT: HOOD RIVER DISTILLERS FIRM: LEOPOLD KETEL & PARTNERS (USA)   **2.** CLIENT: ZSISKA FIRM: MIDNITE OIL (THAILAND)

DESIGNER: MONGKILSRI JANJARASSKUL   **3.** CLIENT: PADDYWAX FIRM: PRINCIPLE (USA) DESIGNERS: PAMELA ZUCCKER AND ALLYSON LACK

4. CLIENT: HOOD RIVER DISTILLERS FIRM: LEOPOLD KETEL & PARTNERS (USA)

1.

2.

1. CLIENT: MONDO USA FIRM: MIRIELLO GRAFICO (USA) DESIGNER: JOSH HIGGINS **2.** CLIENT: TESCO STORES FIRM: R DESIGN (UK)
DESIGNERS: IAIN DOBSON AND SARAH BUSTIN

1.

2.

3.

4.

1. CLIENT: SAN PASQUAL WINERY FIRM: MIRIELLO GRAFICO (SPAIN) DESIGNER: SALLIE REYNOLDS ALLEN **2.** CLIENT: WRIGLEY JR. COMPANY
FIRM: WRIGLEY JR. COMPANY (USA) **3.** CLIENT: ORGANIC COTTAGE FIRM: CRAVE, INC. (USA) DESIGNER: DAVID EDMUNDSON
4. CLIENT: OUTSET, INC. FIRM: OUTSET, INC. (USA) DESIGNER: SARAH OSBORN

1.

2.

3.

4.

1. CLIENT: FREEEZ FIRM: VBAT (NETHERLANDS) DESIGNER: ELKE KUNNEMAN **2.** CLIENT: IQ BEVERAGE GROUP FIRM: CRAVE, INC. (USA)
DESIGNERS: DAVID EDMUNDSON AND RUSS MARTIN **3.** CLIENT: B.T. MCELTRATH FIRM: CAPSULE (USA) DESIGNER: GREG BROSE
4. CLIENT: BISSINGER'S HANDCRAFTED CHOCOLATES FIRM: TOKY BRANDING & DESIGN (USA) DESIGNER: JAMIE BANKS-GEORGE

VERTIKAL premium vodka. 700ml ℮, alc 40% vol.

+ made with highest quality natural spring water vodavoda from banja vrujci source. bottled by si&si company product of serbia and montenegro.

CLIENT: ARTESKA INTERNATIONAL FIRM: NONOBJECT, INC. (USA)

CLIENT: FRITZIE FRESH FIRM: CAPSULE (USA) DESIGNER: HEATHER DONCAVAGE

1.

2.

3.

4.

1. CLIENT: COTT'ITALIA FIRM: R&MAG GRAPHIC DESIGN (ITALY) DESIGNERS: RAFFAELE FONTANELLA, MAURIZIO DI SOMMA, AND MARCELLO CESAR
2. CLIENT: BUNA BET FIRM: VBAT (NETHERLANDS) DESIGNERS: MERIEL VERHEUL AND THEA BAKKER 3. CLIENT: FOURTWENTY FIRM: GOLDFOREST
(USA) DESIGNER: PAT COWAN 4. CLIENT: SHURE INCORPORATED FIRM: COMBINED TECHNOLOGIES, INC. & MIRES+BALL (USA) DESIGNERS: CHUCK
MILLER AND BOB RIZZA

1.

2.

1. CLIENT: SHU UEMURA FIRM: BERGMAN ASSOCIATES (USA) DESIGNERS: ROBERT BERGMAN AND CHRISTOPHE PILLET **2.** CLIENT: ERICKSON LABS
FIRM: CAPSULE (USA) DESIGNER: DAN BAGGENSTOSS

1.

2.

3.

4.

1. CLIENT: SEAFARER BAKING COMPANY FIRM: SABINGRAFIK, INC. (USA) DESIGNER: TRACY SABIN. **2.** CLIENT: BOOTLEG WINES FIRM: TURNER DUCKWORTH (USA) DESIGNER: SHAWN ROSENBERGER **3.** CLIENT: CLICK WINE GROUP FIRM: TURNER DUCKWORTH (UK) DESIGNERS: DAVID TURNER, SHAWN ROSENBERGER, CHRIS GARVEY, BRITTANY HULL, AND RACHEL SHAW **4.** CLIENT: COMPASS FIRM: CAPSULE (USA) DESIGNER: BRIAN ADDUCCI

1.

2.

1. CLIENT: THE OUTDOOR GROUP FIRM: STOCKS TAYLOR BENSON (UK) DESIGNERS: DARRAN SEYMOUR, PAUL BETTS, AND ANDY JACKSON

2. CLIENT: THE SMOKEHOUSE MARKET FIRM: TOKY BRANDING + DESIGN (USA) DESIGNER: JAMIE BANKS-GEORGE

CLIENT: 44° NORTH VODKA FIRM: WALLACE CHURCH, INC. (USA) DESIGNER: CAMILLA KRISTIANSEN

1.

2.

3.

4.

1. CLIENT: HOMEBASE LTD. FIRM: TURNER DUCKWORTH (UK) DESIGNER: MIKE HARRIS **2.** CLIENT: REDHOOK BREWERY FIRM: HORNALL ANDERSON DESIGN WORKS (USA) DESIGNERS: BRUCE STIGLER, ELMER DELA CRUZ, LARRY ANDERSON, BRUCE BRANSON-MEYER, JAY HILBURN, AND BECKON WYLD **3.** CLIENT: APRÈS PEAU CHOCOLATE-TOUR FIRM: WILLOUGHBY DESIGN GROUP (USA) DESIGNERS: STEPHANIE LEE, JESSICA MCENTIRE, AND NATHAN HOFER **4.** CLIENT: SHAKLEE FIRM: TURNER DUCKWORTH (UK) DESIGNER: SHAWN ROSENBERGER

1.

2.

3.

4.

1. CLIENT: COSMETICA FIRM: MIRAN DESIGN (REPUBLIC OF BELARUS) DESIGNER: IGOR SOLOVYOV **2.** CLIENT: AMAZING FOOD WINE FIRM: LIPPINCOTT (USA) DESIGNERS: ALINE KIM AND PETER CHUN **3.** CLIENT: SUPERDRUG STORES PLC FIRM: TURNER DUCKWORTH (UK) DESIGNER: SAM LACHLAN **4.** CLIENT: COCA-COLA FIRM: CAPSULE (USA) DESIGNERS: HEATHER DONCAVAGE AND DAN BAGGENSTOSS

1.

2.

1. CLIENT: ARUBA ALOE ISLAND REMEDY FIRM: LODGE DESIGN COMPANY (USA) DESIGNERS: JARRETT HAGY AND ERIC KASS 2. CLIENT: NAVIGON
FIRM: ROSEFISH (GERMANY) DESIGNERS: ANKE ERDMANN AND GESINE VOSS

1.

2.

3.

4.

1. CLIENT: MEDOYEFF FIRM: FITCH (USA) DESIGNER: RAY UENO 2. CLIENT: 420 SPRING WATER FIRM: THE WILDERNESS (NEW ZEALAND)

DESIGNERS: SIMON OOSTERDIJK AND KELVIN SOH 3. CLIENT: CLICK WINE GROUP FIRM: TURNER DUCKWORTH (UK) DESIGNER: SHAWN

ROSENBERGER 4. CLIENT: 267 INFUSIONS FIRM: 267 INFUSIONS (USA) DESIGNERS: ANOIA JABBARI AND JAEIM JUNG

1.

2.

1. CLIENT: SUPERDRUG STORES, PLC FIRM: TURNER DUCKWORTH (UK) DESIGNER: BRUCE DUCKWORTH **2.** CLIENT: METHOD INC. FIRM: TURNER DUCKWORTH (UK) DESIGNERS: SHAWN ROSENBERGER AND DAVID TURNER

CONTRI

BUTORS

"THE FIRST GREAT GIFT WE CAN BESTOW ON OTHERS IS A GOOD EXAMPLE." — THOMAS MORELL

267 INFUSIONS
Page 178
Designers: Anoia Jabbari & Jaeim Jung
Copywriter: Christina Pacelli
Client: 267 Infusions
USA
www.267.com

ADAM TIHANY/TIHANY DESIGN
Page 66
Art Director: Stark Design
Designers: Daniel Stark & Gaemer Guitierrez
Client: SENCE Rare European
USA

ALOOF DESIGN
Page 63
Art Director: Sam Aloof
Designers: Andrew Scrase & Chris Barham
Photographer: Leigh Simpson
Client: U'Luvka Vodka
UK
www.aloofdesign.com

BENEFIT COSMETICA, LLC
Page 19
Art Director/Designer: Hannah Malott
Copywriter: Benefit Cosmetica, LLC
Client: Benefit
USA
www.benefitcosmetica.com

BERGMAN ASSOCIATES
USA
www.bergassociates.com

Page 154
Art Director/Designer: Robert Bergman
Client: Shu Uemura

Page 171
Art Director/Designer: Robert Bergman
Product Shape Design: Christophe Pillet
Client: Shu Uemura

BLOK DESIGN
Mexico
www.blokdesign.com

Page 16
Art Director: Vanessa Eckstein
Designers: Vanessa Eckstein & Mariana Contegni
Illustrator: Brain Rea
Client: ICC/ R-Earth

Page 60
Art Directors: Vanessa Eckstein (Blok)
& Mark Stoiber (Change)
Designers: Vanessa Eckstein & Patricia Kleeberg
Client: Aspenware/Wun

BRADBURY BRANDING AND DESIGN
Page 162
Art Director/Designer/Illustrator: Catharine Bradbury
Canada
www.bradburydesign.com

BRAND ENGINE
Page 118–121
Art Director: Andrew Otto
Designers: Meghan Zodrow, Andrew Otto, & Konrad Tse
Photographer: Judd Pilossof
Client: Tribeca Kitchen
USA
www.brandengine.com

BRANDIA CENTRAL
Page 73
Art Director: Rui Sampaio de Faria
Designer: José Carlos Mendes
Client: Galp Pluma
Portugal
www.brandiacentral.com

CAHAN & ASSOCIATES
USA
www.cahanassociates.com

Page 16
Art Directors: Bill Cahan & Michael Braley
Designers: Michael Braley
Bottle Design: Todd Simmons
Client: Effen Vodka Bottles

Page 43
Art Director: Bill Cahan
Designer: Erik Adams
Illustrator: John Coultec
Client: Boisset
USA

Page 156
Art Director: Bill Cahan
Designer: Erik Adams
Client: Delicious Brands

CAPSULE
USA
www.capsule.us

Page 13
Art Director: Brian Adducci
Designer: Greg Brose
Client: Capsule

Page 16
Art Director: Brian Adducci
Designer: Dan Baggenstoss
Client: Whitebear Technologies

Page 28–29
Art Director: Brian Adducci
Designers: Dan Baggenstoss & Jenny Stevens
Client: Schroeder Milk

Page 50
Art Director/ Designer/ Illustrator/ Photographer:
Brian Adducci
Client: Compass Marketing

Page 50, 172
Art Director/ Designer: Brian Adducci
Client: Compass

Page 111
Art Director: Brian Adducci
Designer: Greg Brose
Illustrator: Bleach Methane
Photographer: Ellie Kingsbury
Client: Fox River Socks, Inc.

Page 112
Art Director: Brian Adducci
Designer: Greg Brose
Illustrator: Bleach Methane
Client: Fox River Socks, Inc.

Page 113
Art Director: Brian Adducci
Designer: Greg Brose
Illustrator: Bleach Methane
Photographer: Ellie Kingsbury
Copywriter: Elizabeth Saloka
Client: Fox River Socks, Inc.

Page 130–133
Art Director: Brian Adducci
Designers: Brian Adducci & Dan Baggenstoss
Client: Old Nassau Imports

Page 152, 167
Art Director: Brian Adducci
Designer: Greg Brose
Client: B.T. McEltrath

Page 169
Art Director: Brian Adducci
Designer: Heather Doncavage
Client: Fritzie Fresh

Page 171
Art Director: Brian Adducci
Designer: Dan Baggenstoss
Client: Erickson Labs

Page 176
Art Director: Brian Adducci
Designers: Heather Doncavage & Dan Baggenstoss
Client: The Coca-Cola Company

CARLO GIOVANI/DOJO STUDIO
Page 65
Art Director/Designer/Illustrator/
Photographer: Carlo Giovani
Copywriters: Carlo Giovani/ DOJO Studio
Client: DOJO Studio
Brazil
www.carlogiovani.com

CARTER WONG TOMLIN
Page 156
Art Director/ Illustrator: Phil Carter
Designers: Phil Carter & Chloe Vicary
Client: Costa Foods
UK
www.carterwongtomlin.com

CHARGE INDUSTRIAL DESIGN
Page 64
Art Director: Sergio Gedanke
Designers: Sergio Gedanke & Ric Hirst
Client: VitaPlus
USA
www.chargedesign.com

CLIF BAR CREATIVE SERVICES
Page 20
Client: Clif Bar and Company
USA
www.clifbar.com

COMBINED TECHNOLOGIES, INC./
MIRES+BALL
Page 170
Art Directors: Chuck Miller (CTI) & John Ball
(Mires+Ball)
Designers: Chuck Miller & Bob Rizza–CTI
Illustrator: Miguel Perez (Mires+Ball)
Copywriter: Jonathan Stookey (Shure)
Client: Shure Incorporated
USA
www.shure.com

CRAVE, INC.
USA
www.cravebrands.com

Page 159
Art Director: David Edmundson
Designers: Laura Andrews & Russ Martin
Client: The Sugar Plum Fairy Baking Co.

Page 166
Designer: David Edmundson
Client: Organic Cottage

Page 167
Art Director: David Edmundson
Designers: David Edmundson & Russ Martin
Client: IQ Beverage Group

DUSTIN EDWARD ARNOLD
Page 126–129
Art Director/Designer: Dustin E. Arnold
Copywriter: Steve Valentine
Client: LuxeLab
USA
www.dustinarnold.com

ECOIST
Page 20
Art Director: Helen Marcoshamer
Designers: Helen, Yair, and Jonathan Marcoschamer
Client: Ecoist
USA
www.ecoist.com

EVENSON DESIGN GROUP
Page 157
Art Director: Stan Evenson
Designer: Kera Scott
Client: Rocamojo
USA
www.evensondesign

FITCH
Page 13, 178
Art Director/Designer: Ray Ueno
Client: Medoyeff
USA
www.fitch.com

FLEX/THE INNOVATIONLAB
Page 45
Art Director: Jeroen Verbrugge
Designers: Abke Geels & Marc van Zijl
Client: AKZO Nobel
The Netherlands
www.flex.nl

FORMATION DESIGN
Page 44
Art Directors: Stephen McMennamy & Paul Huggett
Designers: Russell Kroll & Paul Huggett
Copywriter: Jerry Cronin
Client: Viz
USA
www.vizdrink.com

FUNNEL: ERIC KASS: UTILITARIAN +
COMMERCIAL + FINE: ART
Page 85, 163
Designer: Eric Kass
Copywriters: Eric Kass & Dori Boneck
Client: Maddy's Organic Meals
USA
www.funnel.tv

FUSEPROJECT
USA
www.fuseproject.com

Page 17
Art Director: Yves Behar
Designers: Yves Behar, Tim Kennedy, & Youjin Nam
Illustrator: Tim Kennedy
Photographer: Marcus Hanschen
Client: Aliph Jawbone Bluetooth Headset

Page 67
Art Director: Yves Behar
Designers: Yves Behar, Johan Liden, & Geoffrey
Illustrator: Johan Liden
Photographer: Marcus Hanschen
Client: Perfume 09

Page 156
Art Director: Yves Behar
Designers: Yves Behar & Tim Kennedy
Illustrator: Tim Kennedy
Photographer: Marcus Hanschen
Client: Herman Miller

GLOJI, INC.
Page 68
Art Director: Peter Kao
Designers: Peter Kao, Zu Yan
Photographer: Kenneth Tang
Client: Gloji, Inc.
USA
www.gloji.com

GOLDFOREST
Page 170
Art Director: Bibiana Pulido
Designer: Pat Cowan
Client: fourtwenty
USA
www.goldforest.com

GRAVITY TANK, INC.
Page 158
Art Director/Copywriter: Robert Zolna
Designers: Scott Ternovits & Moritsugu Kariya
Photographer: Scott Ternovits
Client: OfficeMax
USA
www.gravitytank.com

GREENBLUE
Page 21
Client: GreenBlue
USA
www.greenblue.org

HARRY ALLEN & ASSOCIATES
Page 81
Principal Creative: Harry Allen
Designers: Shawn Booth & Thomas Yu
Photographer: Anton Young
Client: Sonia Kashuk
USA
www.harryallendesign.com

HARCUS DESIGN
Page 156
Art Director: Annette Harcus
Designer: Melonie Ryan
Client: Young & Rubicon
Australia
www.harcus.com.au

HELENA SEO DESIGN
Page 122–125
Art Director/Designer: Helena Seo
Photographer: Bill O'Such
Client: Ineke
USA
www.helenaseo.com

HORNALL ANDERSON DESIGN WORKS
USA
www.hadw.com

Page 70
Art Directors: Jack Anderson & Larry Anderson
Designers: Larry Anderson, Holly Craven, Jay Hilburn,
& Chris Freed
Photographer: Darrell Peterson
Copywriter: Pamela Mason-Davey
Client: Blisscotti

Page 142–145
Art Directors: Jack Anderson & Andrew Wicklund
Packaging Designers: Andrew Wicklund, David Bates,
Elmer dela Cruz, Jacob Carter, Peter Anderson,
& Chris Freed
Copywriter: Sally Bergsen
Client: Microsoft Windows Vista

Page 175
Art Directors: Bruce Stigler & Jack Anderson
Designers: Bruce Stigler, Elmer dela Cruz,
Larry Anderson, Bruce Branson-Meyer, Jay Hillburn,
& Beckon Wyld
Client: Redhook Brewery

HOYNE DESIGN
Australia
www.hoyne.com.au

Page 71
Art Director: Domenic Minieri
Designers: Domenic Minieri & Felicity Davison
Photographer: Marcus Struzina
Client: 11 Fornaio

Page 162
Art Director: Rainer Bulach
Designer: Felicity Davison
Photographer: Marcus Struzina
Client: Foster's Australia

IDEO
Page 21
Art Directors: Ian Grouix & Marc Woollard
Designers: Ian Grouix, Marc Woollard, Amy Leventhal,
Soren DeOrlow, & Phil Stob
Client: Pangea Organics
USA
www.ideo.com

INTERROBANG DESIGN COLLABORATIVE
Page 153
Art Director/Designer: Mark D. Sylvester
Client: TDK Electronics Corp.
USA
www.interrobangdesign.com

KENDALL ROSS
Page 160
Art Directors: David Kendall & Tim Ross
Designer/Illustrator: Charlie Worcester
Client: Made in Washington Stores
USA

KINETIC SINGAPORE
Singapore
www.kinetic.com.sg

Page 42
Art Directors: Pann Lim, Leng Soh, & Roy Poh
Designer/ Illustrator: Leng Soh
Photographer: Jeremy Wong
Copywriter: Eugene Tan
Client: Kinetic Singapore

Page 71
Art Directors/Designers/Illustrators: Roy Poh
& Pann Lim
Copywriter: Alex Goh
Client: Jubes

KOREFE
Page 33
Art Director: Reginald Wagner
Designer: Benjamin Pabst
Copywriter: Sabine Manecke & Alexander Baron
Client: Anthony's Mini Garage Winery
Germany
www.kolle-rebbe.ek

LAURA COE DESIGN ASSOCIATES
Page 13
Art Director: Laura Coe Wright
Designers: Laura Coe Wright & Ryoichi Yotsumoto
Client: Microsoft
USA
www.coedesign.com

LEOPARD KETEL & PARTNERS
Page 161, 164
Art Director: Andrew Reed
Photographer: Michael Jones
Client: Hood River Distillers
USA
www.leoketel.com

LIPPINCOTT
Page 176
Art Director: Connie Birdsall
Designers/Illustrators: Aline Kim, & Peter Chun
Client: Amazing Food Wine
USA
www.lippincott.com

LODGE DESIGN CO.
Page 177
Art Designer: Jarrett Hagy
Designers: Jarrett Hagy & Eric Kass
Copywriter: Jason Roemer
Client: Aruba Aloe Island Remedy
USA
www.lodgedesign.com

MEAT AND POTATOES, INC.
Page 80
Art Directors: TJ River & Todd Gallopo
Designers: TJ River & Johnny Hsu Structure
Design: Ian Dyer, Todd Gallopo, & TJ River
Client: Cabo Wabo Tequila
USA
www.meatoes.com

METHOD PRODUCTS
Page 13, 114–117
Art Director: Stefanie Hermsdorf
Designer: Joshua Handy
Client: Method
USA
www.methodhome.com

MICHAEL OSBORNE DESIGN
USA
www.modsf.com

Page 71
Art Director/Designer: Michael Osborne
Client: Majestic Brands

Page 162
Art Director: Michael Osborne
Designers: Michael Osborne & Alice Koswara
Client: Square One Organic Spirits

MIDNITE OIL
Page 164
Art Director/Designer: Mongkolsri Janjarasskul
Client: ZSISKA
Thailand
www.midniteoil.co.th

MILK LTD.
Page 66
Art Directors: Philip Grube & Ellie Bakopoulou
Client: Vodafone/CU
Greece
www.milk.com.gr

MIRAN DESIGN
Page 176
Art Director/Designer: Igor Solovyov
Photographer: Andei Schukin
Copywriter: Miran Jsc
Client: Cosmetica
www.miran-bel.com

MIRIELLO GRAFICO
USA
www.miriellografico.com

Page 165
Art Director: Dennis Garcia
Designer: Josh Higgins
Photographers: Jeffrey Brown & Mike Smith
Client: Mondo
USA

Page 166
Designer: Sallie Reynolds Allen
Client: San Pasqual Winery

MUGGIE RAMADANI DESIGN STUDIO
Page 53
Art Director/Designer: Muggie Ramadani
Illustrator: Frans Theis
Client: Blumoller A/S
Denmark
www.muggieamadani.com

NICE LTD
Page 152
Art Director: Catherine Chan
Designer/Illustrator: Boksil Kim Choi
Photographer: Steven Kupinski
Client: Procter & Gamble
USA
www.niceltd.com

NONOBJECT, INC.
Page 168
Art Directors: Suncica Lukic & Bronko Lukic
Photographers: Nonobject, Inc. & Nicholas Zurcher
Client: Arteska International
USA
www.nonobject.com

OLD GENERAL STORE PHOTO
Page 14
USA
www.ankenyhistorical.rg

OUTSET, INC.
USA
www.outsetinc.com

Page 135, 137
Art Director/Illustrator: Amy Anderson
Designer/Copywriter/Illustrator: Sarah Osborn
Client: Outset, Inc.

Page 136
Art Director/Photographer/Illustrator: Amy Anderson
Designer/Copywriter/Illustrator: Sarah Osborn
Client: Outset, Inc.

Page 166
Art Director/Photographer: Amy Anderson
Designer/Copywriter/Illustrator: Sarah Osborn
Client: Outset, Inc.

PEARLFISHER
UK
www.pearlfisher.com

Page 155
Art Director/ Designer: Shaun Bowen
Client: Coca-Cola Blak

Page 52
Art Director: Shaun Bowen
Designer: Natalie Chung
Illustrator: Brett Ryder at Heart Agency
Copywriter: Lisa Desforges
Client: Dr. Stuart's

PRINCIPLE
USA
www.designbyprinciple.com

Page 161
Art Directors/Designers: Pamela Zuccker
& Jennifer Sukis
Illustrator: Jennifer Sukis
Client: Paddywax/ Destinations

Page 164
Art Directors/Designers: Pamela Zuccker
& Jennifer Sukis
Client: Paddywax/Journey of the Bee Collection

R DESIGN
Page 165
Art Director: Dave Richmond
Designers: Iain Dobson & Sarah Bustin
Client: Tesco Stores UK
UK
www.r-email.co.uk

REMAG GRAPHIC DESIGN
Page 170
Art Directors/Designers: Raffaele Fontanella,
Maurizio Di Somma, & Marcello Cesar
Client: Cott'Italia
Italy
www.remag.it

REVOLUTION TEA
Page 138–141
Creative Director: Jeff Irish
Designer: Andy Natznick
Photographers: Bob Brody Steve Seymour,
& Dave Tevis
Copywriter: Jill Spear
Client: Revolution Tea
USA
www.revolutiontea.com

ROSEFISH
Page 177
Art Director: Silke Bochat
Designers: Anke Erdmann & Gesine Voss
Client: Navigon
Germany
www.tbwa.de

SABINGRAFIK, INC.
Page 172
Art Director: Bridget Sabin
Designer/Illustrator: Tracy Sabin
Client: Seafarer Baking Company
USA
www.sabin.com

SATELLITE DESIGN
Page 160
Art Director/Designer: Amy Gustincic
Photographer: Adam Clark
Client: The North Face
USA
www.satellite-design.com

SEED
Page 72
Art Director: Mark Walker
Designer: Mark Walker & Garnetteo
Client: Wild Bunch & Co
Singapore
www.seed.uk.com

SMART DESIGN
Page 142–145
Structural Designer/Photographer: Smart Design
Client: Microsoft Windows Vista
USA
www.smartdesignworldwide.com

SMITH & MILTON
Page 13
Art Director: Howard Milton
Designer/ Illustrator: Lee Newham
Copywriter: Lee/Toby
Client: Brody & Stone
UK

SONSOLES LLORENS DISSENY GRAFIC
Page 162
Art Director/ Designer: Sonsoles Llorens
Client: Sans & Sans
Spain
www.sonsoles.com

STOCKS TAYLOR BENSON
Page 173
Designers: Darren Seymour, Paul Betts,
& Andy Jackson
Client: The Outdoor Group
UK
www.stbdesign.com

STUDIOBENBEN
Page 80
Art Director/Designer: Ben Schlitter
Client: TwentyFour Wine
USA
www.benschlitter.com

SUBPLOT DESIGN INC.
Page 32
Art Directors: Matthew Clark & Roy White
Designer: Matthew Clark
Photographer: Waldy Martens
Client: Ryders Eyewear
Canada
www.subplot.com

T.B.D./HATCH DESIGN
Page 152
Art Director: Joel Templin & Gaby Brink
Designer: Katie Jain
Illustrators: Grady McFerrin & Luke Bott
Client: Pepsi
USA
www.hatchsf.com

TOKY BRANDING & DESIGN
USA
www.toky.com

Page 167
Art Director: Eric Thoelke
Designer: Jamie Banks-George
Client: Bissinger's Handcrafted Chocoloates

Page 173
Art Director: Eric Thoelke
Designer: Jamie Banks-George
Client: The Smokehouse Market

TRUE FRUITS GMBH
Page 161
Art Director: Marco Knauf
Designers: Juga Koster & Nicholas Lecloux
Illustrator: Sona Krude
Photographer: Dominik Pietsch
Copywriter: True Fruits GMBH
Germany
www.true-fruits.com

TURNER DUCKWORTH
UK, USA
www.turnerduckworth.com

Page 35
Creative Directors: David Turner & Bruce Duckworth
Designer: Sarah Moffat
Photographer: Andy Grimshaw
Retoucher: Peter Ruane
Artwork: Reuben James
Client: Waitrose Ltd.

Page 35
Creative Directors: David Turner & Bruce Duckworth
Designer: Sam Lachlan
Photographer: Andy Grimshaw
Retoucher: Reuben James
Client: Waitrose Ltd.

Page 35
Creative Directors: David Turner & Bruce Duckworth
Designer: Sam Lachlan
Photographer: Steve Baxter
Retoucher: Peter Ruane
Client: Waitrose Ltd.

Page 49
Creative Directors: David Turner & Bruce Duckworth
Designers: Shawn Rosenberger, Ann Jordan,
Josh Michaels, Rebecca Williams, Brittany Hull,
& Radu Ranga
Structural Designers: BurgoPak & Turner Duckworth
Photo Illustration: Terry Dudley (MOTOKRZR)
& Michael Brunsfeld (MOTOROKR)
Photographer: Lloyd Hryciw (MOTOROKR)
Product Imagery: Paul Obleas, Motorola
Client: Motorola

Page 146–149
Creative Directors: David Turner & Bruce Duckworth
Designers: Sarah Moffat & Chris Garvey
Client: The Coco-Cola Company

Page 157
Creative Directors: David Turner & Bruce Duckworth
Designer: Anthony Biles
Account Manager: Joanne Chan
Client: McKenzie River Corporation

Page 159
Creative Directors: David Turner & Bruce Duckworth
Designer: Anthony Biles
Typographer: Jeremy Tankard & Anthony Biles
Account Manager: Moira Riddell
Client: BOA Housewares

Page 172
Art Director: David Turner & Bruce Duckworth
Designer: Shawn Rosenberger
Photo Illustrator: Jonathon Warner
Client: Bootleg Wines

Page 175
Creative Directors: David Turner & Bruce Duckworth
Designer: Mike Harris
Photographer: David Lidbetter
Retoucher: Peter Ruane
Account Manager: Brad Athay
Client: Homebase Ltd.

Page 175
Creative Directors: David Turner & Bruce Duckworth
Designer: Shawn Rosenberger
Photographer/Illustrator: Danny Smythe
Client: Shaklee

Page 176
Creative Directors: David Turner & Bruce Duckworth
Designer/Typographer: Sam Lachlan
Illustrator: Nathan Jurevicius
Client: Superdrug Stores, Plc

Page 178
Creative Directors: David Turner & Bruce Duckworth
Designer/Illustrator: Shawn Rosenberger
Copywriter: David Turner
Client: Click Wine Group

Page 179
Creative Directors: David Turner & Bruce Duckworth
Designers: Shawn Rosenberger & David Turner
Illustrator: Michael Brunsfeld
Production: Jonathan Warner, Brandy Volmer,
& Laura Pickering
Client: Method, Inc.

Page 179
Creative Directors: David Turner & Bruce Duckworth
Designer: Bruce Duckworth
Illustrator: John Geary
Account Manager: Moira Riddell
Client: Superdrug Stores Plc

TURNSTYLE
Page 36, 84
Art Director/Designer/Illustrator/
Copywriter: Steve Watson
Client: Full Tank
USA
www.turnstylestudio.com

ULFELDT SELLE16
Page 152
Art Director/Designer: Jens Ulfeldt
Photographer: Allison
Client: Scanbech
Denmark
www.selle16.com

WALLACE CHURCH, INC.
USA
www.wallacechurch.com

Page 174
Art Directors: Stan Church & Lawrence Haggerty
Designer: Camilla Kristiansen
Client: 44° North Vodka

Page 161
Art Director: Stan Church
Designer: Marco Escalante
Client: Shango Rum Liqueur

THE WILDERNESS
Page 178
Art Directors/ Designers: Simon Oosterdijk
& Kelvin Soh
Client: 420 Spring Water
New Zealand
www.thewilderness.co.nz

VBAT
The Nethherlands
www.vbat.com

Page 167
Art Director: Rob van Gijzelen
Designer: Elke Kunneman
Photographer: Bart Nijs fotografie
Copywriter: Freeez B.V.
Client: Freeez

Page 170
Art Director: Rob van Gijzelen
Designers : Meriel Verheul & Thea Bakker
Illustrator: Meriel Verheul
Copywriter: James M. Boekbinder
Client: Buna Bet

WILLOUGHBY DESIGN GROUP
Page 175
Art Directors: Ann Willoughby, Nicole Satterwhite,
& Nate Hardin
Designers: Stephanie Lee, Jessica McEntire,
& Nathan Hofer
Photographer: Tim Pott (product photography)
Copywriter: Janette Crawford
Client: Après Peau Chocolate
USA
www.willoughbydesign.com

WEBB SCARLETT DEVLAM
Page 80
Art Directors: Edouard Ball & Sarah Eagan
Designers: Sophie Reynolds & Edward Adomson
Client: Procter & Gamble
Australia
www.wsdv.com

WRIGLEY JR. COMPANY
Page 166
USA
www.wrigley.com

FOR ALL OF YOU WHO HELPED CAPSULE PULL THIS BOOK TOGETHER. CONTRIBUTORS OF WORK WE THANK YOU AND ACKNOWLEDGE YOUR GREAT WORK THROUGHOUT. OTHER CONTRIBUTORS WHO PROVIDED THEIR INSIGHT AND PERSPECTIVE WILLINGLY, WE THANK YOU BELOW.

Greg Zimmer, 3M Company	Andrew Cleveland, Best Buy Company	John DePaolis, Country Choice Organic
Theresa Cosgriff, 3M Company	Bjorn Nabozney, Big Sky Brewing Company	Richard Whitney, Cummins
Judith Grossman, ACCO Brands	Mitch Nash, Blue Q	Curt Aust, Dean Foods
Melissa Smith-Hazen, Ahold USA	Julie Lynn York, Brown Forman	Brian Houck, The Dial Corporation
Nan Bailly, Alexis Bailly Vineyard	Nancy Lucas, Cargill	Dr. Alay Gamay, DreamPak
Jay Glasnapp, Andersen Corporation	Jay Hartman, Cisco Brewers	Jane Casto, Ecolab
James Mathis, Armstrong World Industries	Randy Hudson, Cisco Brewers	Scott Olson, Ecolab
Ashley Rosebrook, Aveda Body Care	Ruth Fowler, Coca-Cola Corporation	Chad Thompson, Ecolab
John Delfausse, Aveda Body Care, and Estée Lauder	David Butler, Coca-Cola Corporation	Mark Pierce, General Mills
Scott Lutz, Best Buy Company	Glenn Geisendorfer, Coca-Cola Corporation	Colleen Dehmer, General Mills
Scott Burglechner, Best Buy Company	L'Anda Flowers, Coca-Cola Corporation	Elizabeth Hocutt, General Mills
Brent Ostrowski, Best Buy Company	Meewha Lee, Colgate-Palmolive	Paul Earl-Torniainen, General Mills
Bart Reed, Best Buy Company	Robert Iredell, Consumer Innovation Partners	Joanna Terhune, Heinz North America

Jeffrey Meier, Honeywell

Lee Green, IBM Corporation

Janine Heffelfinger, Independent Guru

Scott Williams, Morgan Hotels

Ken Giering, Nike

Jill Zanger, Nike

Jim Goddard, Nike

Lorrie Vogel, Nike

Doug Lindenfelser, No Name Steaks

Cassie Pittman, Northern Vineyards Winery

Robert Neufeld, Pfizer

Peter Clark, Product Ventures

Stephen Leonard, SC Johnson

Pat Cappucci, Select Comfort

Brien Martin Wagner, Spray Tech

Steve Prebble, SuperValu

Bruce Tait, TaitSubler

Kim Lymn, Target Corporation

Judy Bell, Target Corporation

Neal Anderson, Target Corporation

Justin Karkoc, Target Corporation

Carol Steele, Target Corporation

Jay Gouliard, Unilever

Sheila Wenke, Unilever

Jay Schrankler, University of Minnesota

Steve Vuolo, University of St. Thomas

Toni Marnul William, Wrigley Jr. Company